LITERACY-AT-WORK BOOK
Reading and Writing Practice

Unit ④ **The Funny Side**

Unit ⑤ **Nature Guides**

Unit ⑥ **It Takes a Leader**

D1457163

Cover Credits: Front Cover: Illustration from "Leopard" from *How the Animals Got Their Colors* by Michael Rosen. Illustration copyright © 1992, 1991 by John Clementson. Reprinted by permission of Harcourt Brace & Company. Interior and Back Covers: Unit 4: Peter Spacek. Unit 5: Dugald Stermer. Unit 6: © Mark Selinger/Outline Jennifer Hazen, 1986.

Copyright © 1996 Scholastic Inc. All rights reserved.   Published by Scholastic Inc.   Printed in the U.S.A.
ISBN 0-590-90696-8
6 7 8 9 10   33   03 02 01

TABLE OF CONTENTS

VOLUME 2

UNIT 4 · THE FUNNY SIDE

UNIT 5 · NATURE GUIDES

UNIT 6 IT TAKES A LEADER

A detailed Table of Contents appears at the start of each unit.

LITERACY-at-WORK
BOOK

The Funny Side

CREATIVE EXPRESSION

TABLE OF CONTENTS

THE FUNNY SIDE

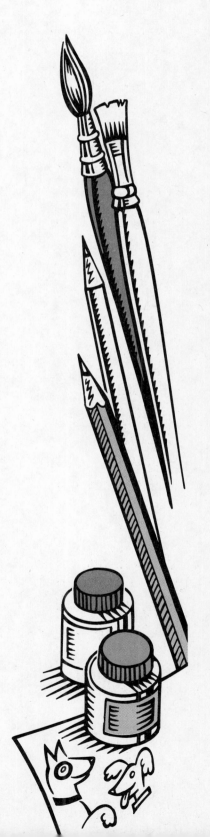

★ NEWSLETTER ★

Welcome to *The Funny Side*

When was the last time you laughed? You'd probably like to do it again soon, right? Everyone likes to laugh. In this section, you'll meet some pretty funny characters and discover how to develop your own funny side. Here's what you'll find inside this SourceBook. So sharpen your funny bone and get ready to laugh.

A Laugh a Day!

You don't have to crack open a joke book to find something to giggle about. Author Judy Blume is great at finding humor in everyday life, and in this section you'll read a story about a peaceful weekend destroyed by a terrible two-year-old. You'll also meet an out-of-this-world professor who thinks Earth humor has gone to the dogs.

Find out why laughing is good for you! + PLUS +

What's So Funny?

In comedy, bigger is sometimes better. You'll read a story by Daniel Pinkwater about a giant chicken, as well as a tall tale about two larger-than-life American heroes.

+ PLUS +

Read some poems and rhymes that will catch you by surprise!

★ NEWSLETTER ★

Funny People

Who's the funniest person you know? The people in this section might compete with your favorite. You'll meet an author and an illustrator who think they're pretty funny. Then you'll read a story about a girl whose right-on riddles stump her brother.

 **The Riddle King will teach you how to create your own riddles.**

Meet Robb Armstrong

This cartoonist uses humor for a serious reason — he tries to teach kids it's cool to stay in school.

Things You'll Do

- "And they all lived wackily ever after". . . or they will, when you write your own *fractured fairy tale.*

- Take the time to find a rhyme as you write some *humorous poetry.*

- Watch out, Snoopy! You'll use pictures and words to create your own *crazy comic strip.*

Let's Visit a Cartoonist's Studio

Visit a real-life funny factory, where you'll find a cartoonist hard at work to keep you chuckling.

Getting Started

HERE are some books you definitely *won't* be reading in this unit. Check out these wacky book titles. Then make up three of your own! Share them with classmates.

- *Under the Umbrella* by April Showers
- *Scary Stories* by Ima Fraid
- *All About the Eiffel Tower* by Ben Tafrance
- *How to Sleep All Day* by I. M. Laizee

WELCOME TO THE CARTOONIST'S STUDIO

1. What's your favorite comic strip or cartoon? Why do you like it?

_____

_____

_____

2. Where do you think a cartoonist gets ideas?

_____

_____

_____

3. What do you want to know about making cartoons?

_____

_____

_____

4. How do you think you could find out more about
   cartoonists and cartooning?

_____

_____

_____

Name

WELCOME TO THE CARTOONIST'S STUDIO

Here's a way to keep track of what you did in the Cartoonist's Studio.

Fill in the chart when you visit the Cartoonist's Studio.

Date	Time Spent	What I Did	What I Learned

SOUNDS LIKE TROUBLE

Complete each sentence with a word from the box.

mumbling: speaking in such a low voice that the words are not understood

cried: shouted loudly

shrieked: made a loud, shrill cry

boomed: made a loud, deep sound

slurping: making a loud sipping sound; drinking noisily

babbling: making sounds that have no meaning

hollered: shouted or called loudly

The picnic planned by our class was going really well until the skunk showed up. Then, all at once…

1. Ricardo _____ so shrilly he sounded like a screeching owl.

2. Amanda _____ so loudly she sounded like a shouting umpire.

3. Our teacher's deep voice _____ like a drum.

4. Mei began _____ like a baby.

5. Matthew was _____ so softly we couldn't understand him.

6. Maria _____ "Go away, skunk!"

7. The skunk just sat there _____ up fruit juice like a thirsty dog.

Describe another scene in which something unexpected happens. Use at least four words from the box.

YOU MAY AS WELL LAUGH

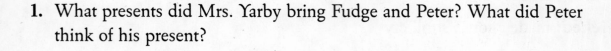

1. What presents did Mrs. Yarby bring Fudge and Peter? What did Peter think of his present?

_____

_____

2. Compare how Mrs. Yarby felt about Fudge when she first met him with how she felt by the end of her visit.

_____

_____

_____

3. How might the story be different if the Yarbys had stayed in a hotel?

_____

_____

4. Explain why you think the author of _Laughing Is Good for You_ might like the story _Mr. and Mrs. Juicy-O._

_____

_____

_____

NARRATIVE: HUMOR

You will write a story about a day that started out like any other but turned out to be surprising and funny. Use the chart to help you.

The day I will write about:

What I expected to happen on this day:

What happened instead:

What was funny about what happened:

My thoughts about this day:

Have I chosen an everyday event that turned into a funny event?
Will there be a funny surprise for the reader?

Name

YARBYS VERSUS HATCHERS

Read each event from "Mr. and Mrs. Juicy-O."
Find something in the story that can be compared
or contrasted with it. Write it in the correct column.

> When you compare two things, ask yourself how they are alike. When you contrast two things, ask yourself how they are different.

EVENT	COMPARISON	CONTRAST
The Yarbys live in Chicago.		
Fudge likes the taste of flowers.		
Fudge's gift is tied with red ribbon.		
Fudge likes his gift.		
Fudge eats dinner alone.		
Mrs. Yarby calls Dribble "that thing."		
Mr. Hatcher dislikes Juicy-O.		

How would the story change if Peter and Fudge were older? Would you be
able to compare and contrast the same things in the story?

Name

BUSTER'S PERFECT DAY

by Rick Landesman

As you read the story, write your questions and ideas about it in the column on the right. Then complete page 10.

My questions and ideas as I read

I had been thinking about that day for a long time. Most kids just wait for the first day of summer. Not me. I *plan* for it. "The plan" for this perfect day looked like this:

Stage 1: Morning — sleep in and read comic books.

Stage 2: Afternoon — bike with Katie to Horseshoe Lake.

Stage 3: Night — have a picnic at our house; catch fireflies and play hide-and-seek; read a mystery book in bed.

Unfortunately, I forgot to tell Buster about "the plan." Buster is my little sister Peg's dog. I like dogs, but he doesn't count. Buster is big. Buster is smelly. Buster is a pest. The real problem is, I don't like him, but he *loves* me. He follows me around and does everything he can to ruin my life. He made my perfect day into a perfect disaster. Here's how it went:

Stage 1: Sleep in. Forget it! Buster jumped on me at sunrise. Mom said he was just being friendly. Some friend.

Stage 2: A nice bike ride? Nope! Mom had to take Buster to the vet, and I had to stay home to watch Peg. Buster ruined a whole afternoon without even being there.

Stage 3: Well, we had the picnic. It was great, but hide-and-seek was another Buster special. He trailed me to every hiding place and barked whenever I stopped moving. I was "it" all night. Finally, I was curled up in bed with my book. I was about to find out who did it when — well, you can guess. *Buster* did it. He ate the book.

Name

COMPARE/CONTRAST

Read "Buster's Perfect Day." Compare and contrast some of the narrator's plans with what actually happened.

When you compare and contrast characters and events, ask, How are these things similar? How are they different?

	What the Narrator Planned	What Really Happened	Comparison or Contrast
Morning			
Afternoon			
Night			
Night			

Tell about a day, like the one in "Buster's Perfect Day," when nothing seemed to go the way you planned it. Compare and contrast what you planned with what really happened.

ANNOUNCE A NEW CARTOON CHARACTER

How can you announce the "birth" of a new cartoon character? By sending a birth announcement! Fill in the announcement below for a new character you've created or for a favorite character who already exists. If you like, draw a picture, too.

CARTOONIST'S STUDIO

ANNOUNCING THE BIRTH OF

BORN:

NOW APPEARING IN:

FIELD TRIP TO EARTH

Fill in each blank with the correct word from the box to get all the information you need to go on the trip to Earth.

deadline: the latest time by which something has to be completed

career: a profession or occupation that a person does through life

organized: arranged in an orderly way

competitive: working against others for the same prize or goal

self-disciplined: controlling oneself

development: the act of creating something new

INSTRUCTIONS

Our field trip to Earth is in two weeks. Monday is the last day for bringing in trip fees.

Don't miss the (1) _____. You may have to give up your habit of having an

afternoon treat. To save enough money, you'll need to be (2) _____.

This trip is a great opportunity if you want to make the study of Earthlings your life's

(3) _____. Since many others are interested in this line of work, you

must be (4) _____ to succeed at it. During the long flight, work on the

(5) _____ of a plan to explore Earth. Remember that you must be

(6) _____: clothing in one bag and equipment in another. And don't forget

all three of your mittens.

You are leading a tour of planet Earth. Use at least three words from the box to describe how Earthlings behave.

MAKING FUN

1. Why did Robb Armstrong decide to be a cartoonist?

_____

_____

_____

_____

2. Is being a cartoonist as easy as Robb thought it would be when he started out? Why or why not?

_____

_____

_____

_____

3. Where does Robb Armstrong get ideas for his cartoon strips?

_____

_____

_____

_____

4 How is the situation in _Earth Hounds_ similiar to the situations that Robb Armstrong uses when he creates a comic strip?

_____

_____

_____

_____

REAL-LIFE LAUGHS

Robb Armstrong gets his funny ideas from everyday life.
Think of something funny that has happened to you or to someone you know.
Draw a picture based on the event, and give it a wacky caption. See if your
cartoon can make someone laugh!

CARTOON

Use the panels below to jot down ideas for a cartoon strip. Think about how you can add exaggeration and surprise to the humor.

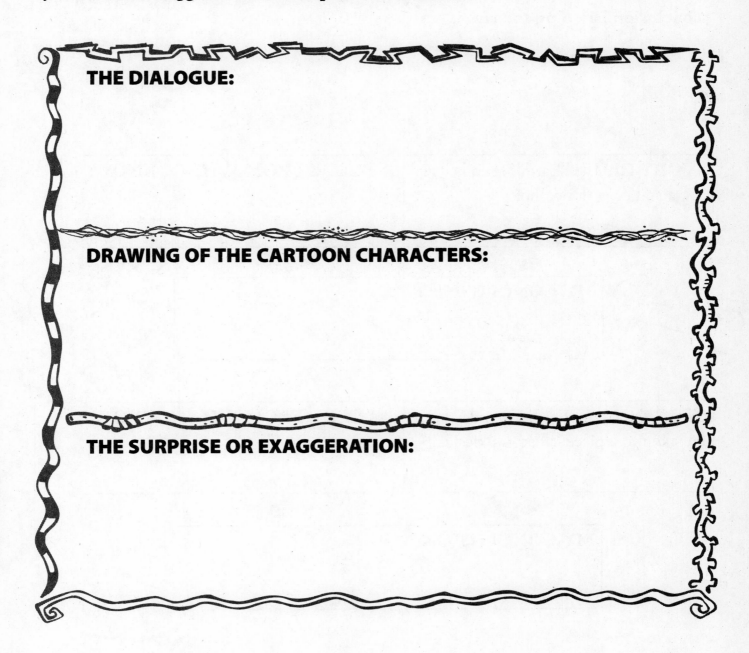

THE DIALOGUE:

DRAWING OF THE CARTOON CHARACTERS:

THE SURPRISE OR EXAGGERATION:

Is the cartoon strip easy to understand?

Have I included a surprise or exaggeration?

BONE UP ON DOGS

Read each clue from *Earth Hounds*. Use what you know to write another clue. Then draw a conclusion based on the clues.

> Draw conclusions when an author does not spell out everything you want to know about a character or an event.

STORY CLUE: "Earth Hounds have . . . a sniffer with two holes . . ."	CLUE FROM WHAT I KNOW:

MY CONCLUSION:

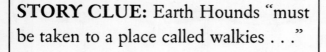

STORY CLUE: Earth Hounds "must be taken to a place called walkies . . ."	CLUE FROM WHAT I KNOW:

MY CONCLUSION:

 Do you think the author of *Earth Hounds* likes dogs? Use story clues and what you know to support your conclusion.

SPARKY AND SAL

by R. T. Tyler

Read this cartoon. Use it to complete page 18.

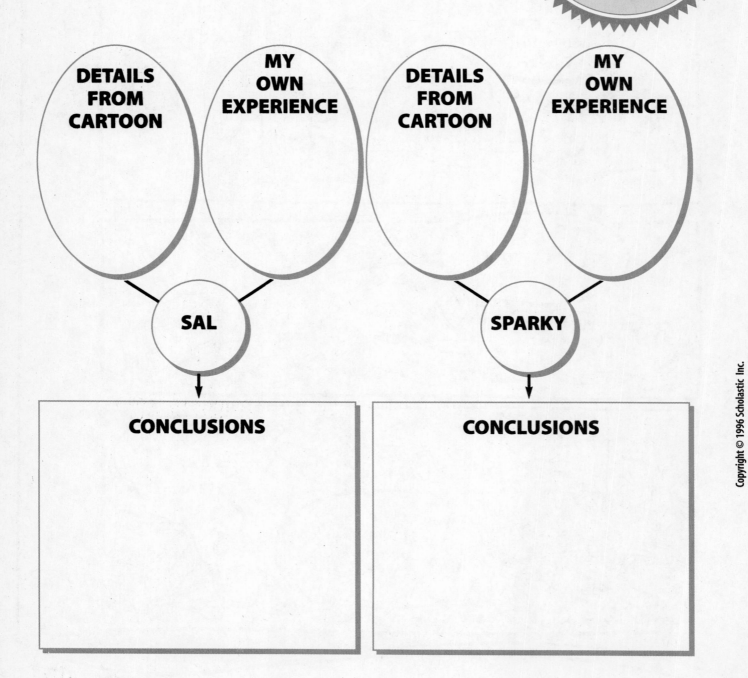

Name

DRAW CONCLUSIONS

In the ovals, jot down notes about the two characters in "Sparky and Sal." Then use your notes to draw conclusions about each character.

When you draw conclusions, look for places in a story where an author does not spell out everything about a character or an event.

| DETAILS FROM CARTOON | MY OWN EXPERIENCE | DETAILS FROM CARTOON | MY OWN EXPERIENCE |

SAL

SPARKY

CONCLUSIONS

CONCLUSIONS

WHICH ONE IS IT?

**Read each pair of sentences about *Earth Hounds*.
Circle the words that correctly complete the
statements that follow.**

> Homophones
> sound the same but have
> different spellings.
> Homographs
> have the same spelling
> but different
> meanings.

1. (a) <u>For</u> dinner, Hounds eat meat.
   (b) They eat socks that are <u>four</u> days old.

    The word meaning "one more than three" is   for   four

    The word meaning "serving as" is   for   four

2. (a) Hounds <u>can</u> stand on two legs.
   (b) Sometimes their meal comes in a <u>can</u>.

    Can means "to be able to" in   sentence a   sentence b

    Can means "a metal container" in   sentence a   sentence b

3. (a) Houndlets always <u>read</u> newspapers that are on the floor.
   (b) I once <u>read</u> that they sleep in Earthling's nocturnal footwear.

    Read means "to look at written words and understand
    their meaning" in   sentence a   sentence b

    Read means "looked at written words and understood
    their meaning" in   sentence a   sentence b

4. (a) The Earthling finds a <u>piece</u> of tree.
   (b) Earthlings like a little <u>peace</u> and quiet.

    Piece means "a part of" in   sentence a   sentence b

    Peace means "calmness" in   sentence a   sentence b

Write your own description of Earth Hounds.
Use a pair of homophones or homographs.

HOMOPHONES/HOMOGRAPHS

Complete each sentence about "Sparky and Sal" on page 17. Write the correct homophone or homograph in the blank. Then write a sentence using the other homophone or homograph.

Homophones sound alike but have different spellings and meanings. Homographs are spelled the same way but have different meanings and pronunciations.

HOMOGRAPHS
record, record
saw, saw

HOMOPHONES
hear, here
knot, not
knead, need

1. To walk a dog, you _____ a leash.

   _____

2. Sal _____ the leash sticking out from under a pile of clothes.

   _____

3. _____ is the leash!

   _____

4. Sal set a new _____ by not cleaning her room for two months.

   _____

5. Sparky would _____ hold his breath while waiting for Sal.

   _____

 Write two headlines about "Sparky and Sal." Use a pair of homophones in one and a pair of homographs in the other.

NAME THAT 'TOON!

Cartoonists get their ideas from many places—even from the letters in their own names! Look at the cartoon character made from the name "Luis." Then draw your own cartoon character, using the letters or initials in your name.

CARTOONIST'S STUDIO

How Does It End?

Below, you'll find a fractured fairy tale without an ending.

Read the story. Then finish the story by writing your own ending on the bottom of this sheet. Use another sheet of paper if you need it.

CINDERELLA'S SLIPPER TELLS ALL

"No one ever hears my side of the story," said Cinderella's right slipper to the reporter, "but things were hard for me, too." This is Ms. Slipper's story.

Ms. Slipper came into the world on the eve of a glamorous ball with her ideal partner beside her. She and Mr. Slipper were to attend the ball together in a glorious coach. "Not only did it have four white horses and footmen, which everybody knows about," said Ms. Slipper, "but it had the thickest carpeting inside that you ever dug your soles into."

The slippers glided around the dance floor for hours. But then it happened: the clock began chiming midnight. "Well," explained Ms. Slipper, "off Cindy ran, past the fancy guards and down the marble stairs, without a thought for our well-being." That's when she lost Mr. Slipper.

For days Ms. Slipper lay locked inside a dark drawer, worrying about her partner. "He could have been lying in a ditch somewhere!" exclaimed Ms. Slipper.

At long last, the Prince arrived with Mr. Slipper. (Ms. Slipper knew this because she peeked out of the keyhole in the drawer.) "Go!" Ms. Slipper said to Cindy. "Go! Show them it's your slipper!" But Cinderella was too busy polishing the fireplace tools.

So, the big-footed sister was the first to try on the shoe. "Oh! I thought that big foot would break him for sure!" wailed Ms. Slipper as she told her tale.

Then the little-footed sister tried on the shoe. "The way she dragged him around the room was silly. She could have broken off his heel."

_____

_____

_____

_____

GREAT STORIES, GREAT ENDINGS

Think back to the fractured fairy tale you completed on page 22. Did you enjoy it? Would you recommend it to your friends?

Answer the following questions about the fractured fairy tale.

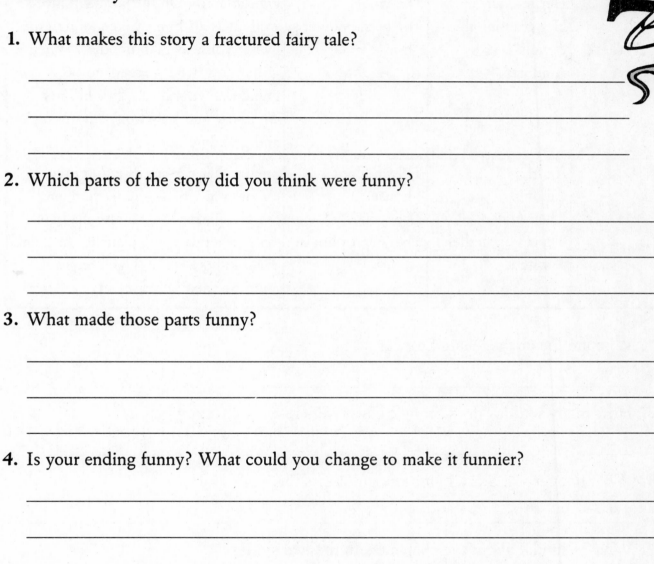

1. What makes this story a fractured fairy tale?

_____

_____

_____

2. Which parts of the story did you think were funny?

_____

_____

_____

3. What made those parts funny?

_____

_____

_____

4. Is your ending funny? What could you change to make it funnier?

_____

_____

_____

USE CHARTS AND TABLES

Story charts can help you see, at a glance, the most important elements of a tale. For example, here is a story chart comparing two fairy tales.

	CHARACTERS	SETTING	EVENTS
STORY 1	A girl Her mother Her grandmother A wolf A hunter	The girl's house The woods The grandmother's house	Girl's mother sends her to visit grandmother. On the way, girl meets wolf and tells him where grandmother lives. Wolf eats grandmother. When girl arrives, wolf pretends to be grandmother and eats girl. Hunter comes by and kills wolf; out jump girl and grandmother.
STORY 2	A girl A boy Their father Their stepmother A witch	The children's house The woods The witch's house	Stepmother convinces father to take children to woods and leave them there. Children find house made of cake, where a witch plans to eat them. They kill the witch, take her jewels, and find their father again.

1. Who are the characters in Story 1?

   _____

2. How many settings does Story 2 have? Where does the story begin?

   _____

3. What happens in Story 1 after the girl meets the wolf?

   _____

4. What is similar about the characters in the two stories?

   _____

5. Do the stories have sad or happy endings?

   _____

THE CAT COMES HOME

Read the story, then fill in each blank with the word from the box that best completes the sentence.

frazzled: emotionally or physically worn out

indignantly: in an angry, scornful way

speechless: unable to speak for a moment

beseechingly: in a begging, pleading way

STRAY-CAT BLUES

Coming home yesterday, I met a cat. It looked (1) _____, as if it were

homeless and tired of its hard life. I would have walked on, but the creature mewed

and looked at me (2) _____. I decided it was

begging, so I let it follow me home. When Grandma came in and

saw the cat, she was so angry she was (3) _____ .

Then she recovered her voice. "Who brought that cat into the

house?" she asked (4) _____. The cat looked at

Grandma and mewed sadly. Finally Grandma sighed

and said, "All right, we'll let this one stay. But

this is the last stray cat we're adopting."

What other words can you think of that would fit in each blank space in the story? Rewrite the story, using different words. Describe how the meaning of the story changed.

WHAT ABOUT CHICKEN?

1. How do you know it's important to have a turkey for Thanksgiving?

   _____

   _____

2. How are Professor Mazzocchi's chickens different from ordinary chickens?

   _____

   _____

3. Why do you think Arthur bought the super chicken?

   _____

   _____

   _____

4. What does Momma tell Poppa to convince him to let Arthur keep the chicken for a pet?

   _____

   _____

   _____

5. What are some of the unexpected surprise twists in *The Hoboken Chicken Emergency* and *Poems of A. Nonny Mouse*?

   _____

   _____

   _____

TELEVISION SCRIPT

You will write a script based on something that really happened to you and a friend or family member. First, decide on the setting and characters. Then, on each screen, jot down ideas for a scene. Include some ideas for what the characters will say in each scene.

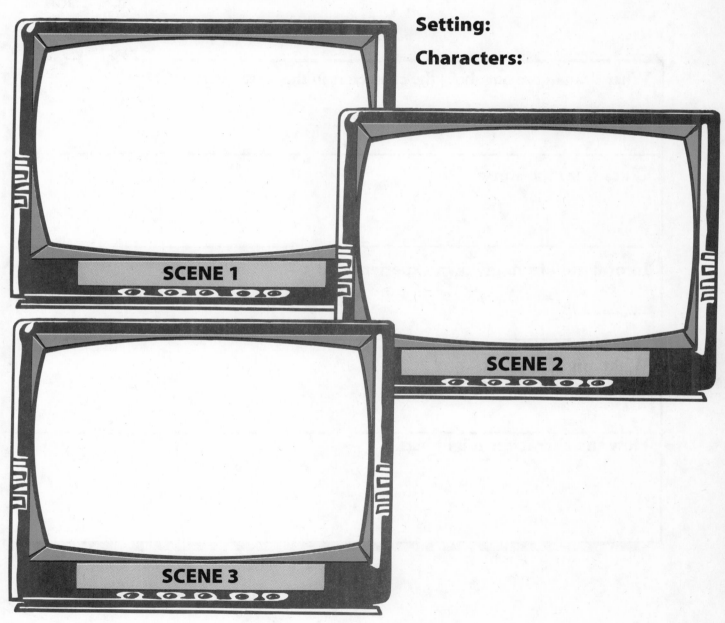

Setting:

Characters:

SCENE 1

SCENE 2

SCENE 3

Is my story idea based on something that really happened to me?

Have I described the setting and the characters?

Have I suggested ideas for what the characters will say?

I MIGHT HAVE KNOWN!

Use what you can figure out about the characters to come up with an idea for another scene in the screenplay *The Hoboken Chicken Emergency*. Use the chart below to plan your scene.

To make inferences, ask yourself, "What is the author leaving out that is important to understanding the character or the event?"

What I can figure out about the characters in the screenplay:
Clues from the story:
Information from my own experience:
What might happen:
How the characters might act:

What information can you figure out about Daniel Manus Pinkwater, the author of *The Hoboken Chicken Emergency*? What clues support this information?

Copyright © 1996 Scholastic Inc.

SISTER FROM ANOTHER PLANET

by Rita Rodriguez

Read this script. Then use it to complete page 30.

Monica and Lena's Bedroom—Night

Lena and Monica are in their bedroom. They are both wearing flannel pajamas. Lena is asleep. Monica is in bed, reading. Suddenly, she laughs very loudly. Lena wakes up, startled.

Lena: What is it?

Monica: The giant space llama ate the evil scientists. Now it's going to eat the hero!

Lena: The giant space llama?

Monica: It's in this book, *Space Llamas From Neptune.* You've got to read it!

Lena: *(impatiently)* Go to sleep and shut the window. It's cold, and besides, the space llama might climb in and eat you.

Lena rolls over and pulls up her blanket. Monica keeps reading. Lena gets out of bed. Monica doesn't notice her. Lena creeps over to Monica and grabs her by the shoulders. Monica, taken by surprise, screams.

Monica: You think you're pretty funny, don't you?

Lena: *(laughing)* You were so worried about evil space llamas that you forgot you were in the same room with the "Sister From Another Planet."

Lena climbs back into bed.

Monica: *(laughing)* OK, OK. You win. Good night, "Sister From Another Planet."

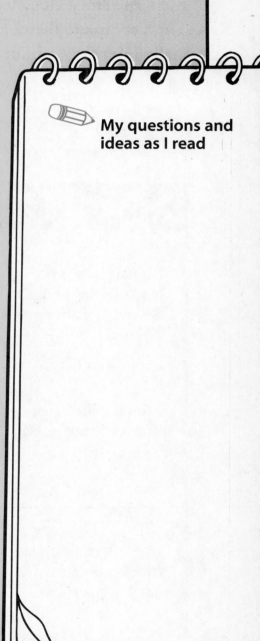

My questions and ideas as I read

Name

MAKE INFERENCES

Read the story clues from "Sister From Another Planet."
Then complete the chart by using what you know to
make inferences about the characters.

When you make inferences, you decide what the author is leaving out that is important to understanding a character or event.

STORY CLUE		WHAT I KNOW		INFERENCE
Monica laughs out loud while reading *Space Llamas From Neptune*.	+		→	
Monica tells Lena, "You've got to read it!"	+		→	
Lena plays a harmless trick on Monica. They laugh.	+		→	

Write another scene for "Sister From Another Planet." Use inferences
from the script on page 29 to help you decide what each character will do.

SHOW ME!

You are the set designer for *The Hoboken Chicken Emergency*. Choose one setting—the Bobowicz's living room, the Hoboken street where Arthur goes to buy the turkey, or Professor Mazzocchi's apartment. In the space below, describe the setting.

Identify the setting by looking for information about the surroundings, clothing, weather, and other details.

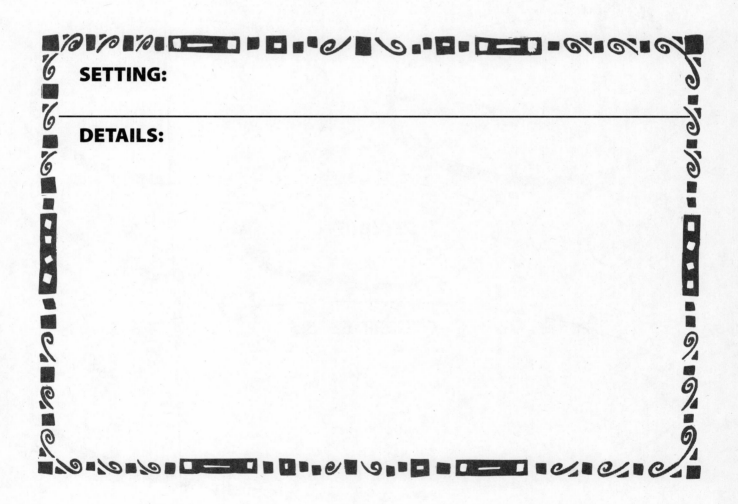

SETTING:

DETAILS:

Think of a setting. Write a list of clues to describe it. Then challenge a classmate to read the clues and guess the setting.

SETTING

Use the web to examine the setting of "Sister From Another Planet" on page 30.

Setting is the place and time of a story. To identify place, look for buildings and surroundings. To identify time, look for clothing, weather, and other details.

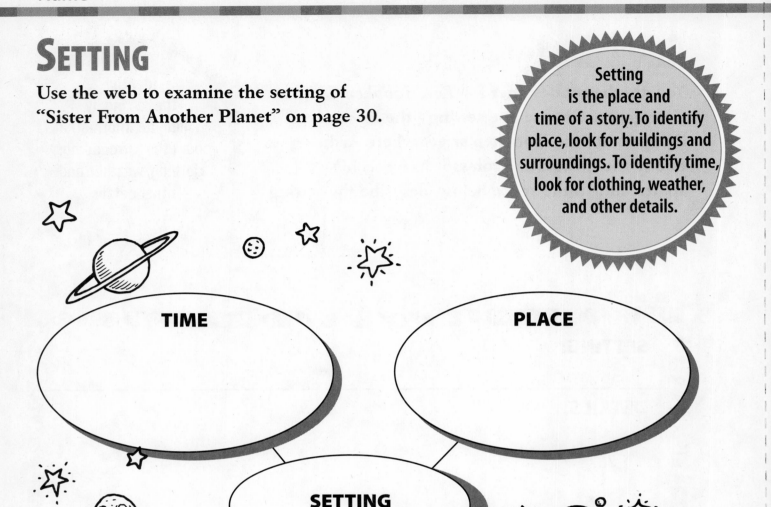

TIME

PLACE

SETTING

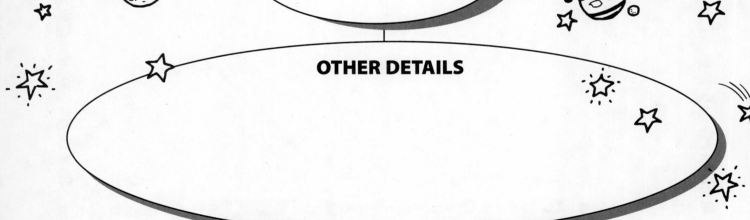

OTHER DETAILS

Imagine you are continuing the play "Sister From Another Planet." Describe the setting of another scene.

MAKE A FLIP-BOOK

Before animation and movies were invented, people could make figures move by using flip-books. How would you finish the flip-book on this page? Draw the missing pages. Then cut the pages apart, staple the side of the book, and flip the pages.

CARTOONIST'S STUDIO

A HEROINE ON THE FRONTIER

Complete the answer to each question with a word from the box.

heroine: a woman admired for her bravery and courage

frontier: the farthest settlement next to an unexplored region

fictional: made-up or imaginary

varmint: person or animal considered troublesome

reputation: character, fame, status

incident: something that happens

1. After Wild West Wanda pulled 12 covered wagons out of quicksand, how did the settlers describe her? They called her a _____.

2. When Wanda went exploring beyond the last settlement in the region, where did she go? She entered the _____.

3. After Wanda scared off the troublesome rabbit, what did she say? "That's all we'll see of that _____."

4. Why didn't Wanda worry when a boulder rolled down the mountain, coming right at her? She thought it was a minor _____.

5. Why did the new settlers think Wanda was brave even though they'd never met her? She had a _____ for bravery.

6. When Gerard told Kenisha about Wild West Wanda, what did Kenisha say? "No such person ever lived. I think she is _____."

 Find pictures in a magazine that illustrate at least three words from the box. Make up captions using the words.

BIGGER THAN LIFE

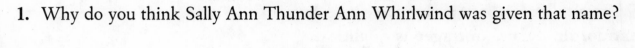

1. Why do you think Sally Ann Thunder Ann Whirlwind was given that name?

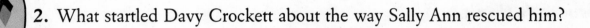

_____

_____

2. What startled Davy Crockett about the way Sally Ann rescued him?

_____

_____

3. Davy Crockett called Sally Ann "Sweetie." Did she like that? Why or why not?

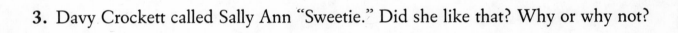

_____

_____

_____

4. In both _The Talking Mule_ and _Sally Ann Thunder Ann Whirlwind_, characters do things that they could not do in real life. What are some of the unlikely things the characters in the two stories do?

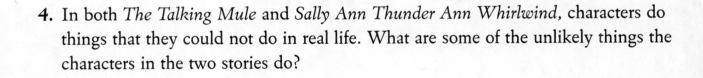

_____

_____

_____

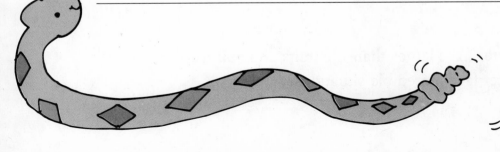
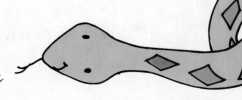

TALL TALE: CHARACTER

Write a tall tale about a character who has
extraordinary and outrageous qualities.
Use the chart below to help you.

Character's Name:

Outrageous Qualities:

Physical features:

Mental abilities:

Incredible talents:

Outrageous Situations the Character Will Face:

Does my character have larger-than-life traits and abilities?
Will my character face incredible situations?

Name

THE ORDER OF EVENTS

Each sentence below signals an event in "Sally Ann Thunder Ann Whirlwind." Read the sentences, and number them from 1 to 6 to indicate their story order. Underline all signal words you find.

To figure out the sequence of events, look for words such as *first, then, next, suddenly, at the same time, before ,* and *after.*

☐ Suddenly, it began to rain and Davy Crockett sat down under a tree to keep from getting wet.

☐ When Davy Crockett woke up, he discovered that his head had gotten stuck in a tree.

☐ One spring day, Davy Crockett went into the forest to hunt for bears.

☐ The woman tied together a bunch of rattlesnakes and used them as a rope to pull the branch away from Davy Crockett's head.

☐ Then a woman came along and saw Davy Crockett struggling with the tree.

☐ Pretty soon, Davy Crockett fell asleep.

Write a recipe for Sally Ann Thunder Ann Whirlwind's dumplings or for something else Sally Ann might have cooked. Be sure to show the order of events that must be followed.

A Shark Named Rover

by Gina Lewis

As you read the story, write your questions and ideas about it in the column on the right. Then complete page 39.

Most people pick dogs or cats or parakeets for pets, but the best pet I ever had was a shark. Of course, the first time he swam up to our boat, I was pretty scared. He had more teeth in his mouth than a tree has leaves. But next he wiggled his fin and I couldn't resist. Mom said I could keep him as long as he didn't get the carpet wet.

I named him Rover, and we had lots of fun together. However, the neighbors started to get a little nervous once they heard I had a pet shark. They didn't want their kids playing with a shark. Then I got a great idea. Rover and I went door to door to share his services as a knife sharpener and can opener. His teeth were so sharp he could open a can by just smiling at it. He could sharpen a knife by licking it.

That's when everyone agreed that Rover was a fine neighbor. They did ask me to tie a red bandanna around his neck so that no one would confuse him with another, less friendly shark. If only Rover hadn't loved boats so much. He was always chasing them, until finally he went after a brand-new speedboat. No one's seen him since. So if you spot a shark in a red bandanna, please tell him to come home. We miss him.

My questions and ideas as I read

Name

SEQUENCE

Read "A Shark Named Rover" on page 38. Then complete the chart by writing five events from the story in their correct sequence. Notice any signal words that give you clues to the order of events.

To help you figure out the sequence of events in a story, look for signal words such as *first, then, next, suddenly, at the same time, before,* and *after.*

First:

Next:

After that:

Then:

Finally:

Write a sequence of events telling what might happen if the narrator finds Rover.

Name

SALLY AND THE DANCING BEAR

In the following sentences, the parts of the plot—the problem, the attempt to solve the problem, the solution, and the result—are out of order. In the box before each sentence, write a number between 1 and 4 to show the order the events happened. In the box after the sentence, write which part of the plot the sentence represents.

To figure out the plot, ask yourself, What is the problem in the story? What events lead to the solution? What is the solution?

☐ Sally asks Great King Bear to dance. ☐

☐ Sally gives Great King Bear a dumpling. ☐

☐ Sally ties a string from Great King Bear's ankle to her churn, so she and the bear will churn the butter as they dance. ☐

☐ Great King Bear wants to steal a smoked ham from Sally's kitchen. Then he wants to eat Sally. ☐

Think about why all the parts of the plot are important. Write what you think "Sally Ann Thunder Ann Whirlwind" would be like if the author had left out one of the parts.

Name

PLOT

In each box below, write an important event from "A Shark Named Rover" on page 38 that makes up the story plot. The plot of the story shows what happens in the story.

To figure out the plot, ask, "What is the problem in the story? What events lead to the solution? What is the solution?"

PROBLEM:

$+$

SOLUTIONS:

$=$

STORY OUTCOME:

The problem at the end of "A Shark Named Rover" is that Rover swims away. Using this as the basis for your plot, write a paragraph about the events following Rover's disappearance.

DESIGN A LETTERHEAD

Some letter paper is printed with a person's name and address—it's called a letterhead. Cartoonists often make their letterheads special by adding their artwork.

Look at the example below. Then make your own letterhead with your name, address, and art that tells about you.

1447 South Lake Avenue
Pasadena, CA 91101

WRITE A POEM

Any everyday situation can be the inspiration for a poem. Look at the cartoon below.
How could you turn it into a funny poem? Think about the form of your poem.
Do you want the lines to be long or short? Do you want the poem to rhyme?

**First, make a list of words that describe the dog and what it is doing.
Try to use some funny-sounding words. Then, put these words
together to write a short poem.**

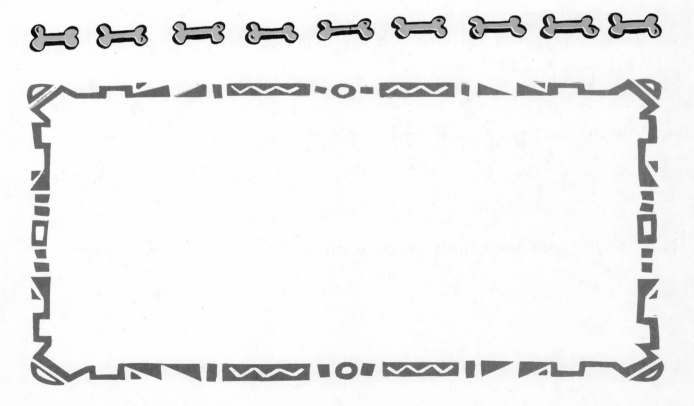

IMPROVE YOUR POEM

Look back at the poem you wrote.
Do you think you could make it better?

1. Does the poem make you see the dog in
   the cartoon? What words could you add to
   make the image more vivid?

   _____

   _____

   _____

2. Does the poem make you laugh? What words could you add to make
   it sound funnier?

   _____

   _____

3. Would the poem be funnier if it were written in a certain shape?
   What shape would you like to use?

   _____

4. What else could you do to improve the poem?

   _____

   _____

Now rewrite your poem in the space below or on a separate sheet of paper.

Name

USE A THESAURUS

A thesaurus is a handy book that contains an alphabetical listing of words and their synonyms and antonyms.

> **funny** adj. causing laughter or amusement
> *syn.* amusing, comical, droll, humorous, laughable, hilarious, ridiculous
> *ant.* dull, dismal, mournful, sad, serious, solemn, cheerless

Use the sample thesaurus entry above to answer the following questions.

1. What are three synonyms for the word *funny*?

   _____

2. What are three antonyms for *funny*?

   _____

3. The word *funny* is what part of speech?

   _____

4. What are three synonyms for the word *sad*?

   _____

5. In the Workshop, you wrote a funny poem. What else could you call it, using synonyms for both *funny* and *poem*? The following words are synonyms for the word *poem*: *verse, rhyme, song, jingle, ballad, limerick.*

   _____

Rewrite the following sentence. Replace each underlined word with a different synonym from the entry above.

The <u>funny</u> clown, dressed in a <u>funny</u> polka-dotted costume, delivered a <u>funny</u> performance.

   _____

   _____

ARTWORKS

Read the words in the box and their definitions. Then look at the groups of words below. Write a sentence, using all the words in each group.

doodled: scribbled or drew without paying attention

cartoon characters: people or animals that are humorously drawn

artwork: works of art

animated: showing movement or action

media: different kinds of materials used to create artwork

illustration: a picture or diagram used to decorate or explain something

collage: a picture made by gluing different kinds of materials to a surface

creative: artistic, inventive, original

1. collage • artwork • media

_____

_____

2. illustration • creative

_____

3. doodled • animated • cartoon characters

_____

_____

You are taking an art class. In a letter to a friend, explain the kinds of things you are making. Use four of the words from the box.

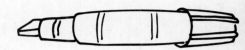
SAYING IT THROUGH PICTURES

1. Name one event that encouraged Lane Smith to become an artist.

_____

_____

_____

2. Lane Smith draws with humor. He also tells a story with humor. What is one funny thing he tells about?

_____

_____

_____

3. Why do you think Lane Smith dedicated one of his books to Mr. Baughman?

_____

_____

_____

4. Jon Sciezka and Lane Smith have a similar sense of humor. What are some examples of their humor?

_____

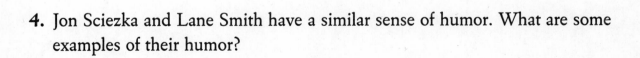

_____

_____

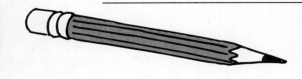

WRITER'S STYLE

You will write a funny story in which a very strange thing
happens at an ordinary event. Use the chart to brainstorm
wild ideas. Remember: Reality doesn't count!

Weird Characters	Funny Names	Strange Happenings

Will the story make readers laugh?
Is there at least one weird character?
Will the writing contain any slapstick humor?

Name

IN MY OPINION

Read the following sentences from "Lane Smith." Check the box to show that you agree or disagree with each statement. Explain your opinion on the lines provided. To support your answer, include information you knew before you read the selection or evidence from the selection.

Use your own experience to make judgments about what you read.

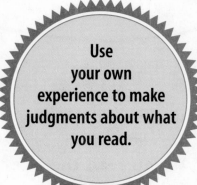

1. "You see, all cartoon characters are made up primarily of circles."

☐ I agree ☐ I do not agree

Here's why: _____

2. "I learned that different media could create different moods."

☐ I agree ☐ I do not agree

Here's why: _____

3. "Watercolors make great sad-rainy-day pictures."

☐ I agree ☐ I do not agree

Here's why: _____

4. "To be an artist you have to keep on doing art—just draw, draw, draw!"

☐ I agree ☐ I do not agree

Here's why: _____

THINK & WRITE

Do you agree that it is a good thing Lane Smith didn't become a mathematician? What evidence can you give to support your judgment?

A WRITER SPEAKS

Interview with Eleanora E. Tate, from "Popcorn Pumps Up Tate's Imagination": _Storyworks_

As you read the interview, write your questions and ideas about it in the column on the right. Then complete page 51.

Author Eleanora E. Tate began writing in the third grade. She wrote a story about giant amoeba monsters. Now she is grown up and has written five books for kids. Ms. Tate is also president of the National Association of Black Storytellers.

Where do you get ideas?
From the people around me. Then I have to make them larger than life so that people will want to read my work.

Where can kids find story ideas?
Go to the library. Go to your grandmothers, uncles, next-door neighbors, aunts, and listen.

What advice do you give to kids who are writers?
You all have messages to give to the world. Write your stories down first. Don't worry too much about spelling and punctuation on the first draft. Remember that most stories have a beginning, a middle, an end, a character, a problem, and a description of how that character tries to solve that problem.

When you're writing a story, how long does it take?
It seems I go through millions of drafts. Before the book is completely done, I've probably rewritten every word seven times. My husband faithfully reads every word. I don't often have other people read my work while I'm in the process. It's like tasting the cake before it comes out of the oven.

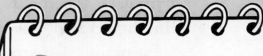

 My questions and ideas as I read

"Popcorn Pumps Up Tate's Imagination" from STORYWORKS® Fall 1992. Copyright © 1992 by Scholastic Inc. Reprinted by permission. Copyright © 1996 Scholastic Inc.

MAKE JUDGMENTS

Read "A Writer Speaks." Then, using your own experience, complete the chart by making judgments about what Eleanora E. Tate says.

The fact that something is in print doesn't necessarily make it true. Use your own experience to make judgments about what you read.

Tate says that we can go to people we know and to the library to find ideas for stories. She says it's important to listen.

My Experience

My Judgment

Tate says that she goes through millions of drafts before a book is done.

My Experience

My Judgment

Write three questions you would ask Eleanora E. Tate. What judgments do you think you could make from her answers?

PRE-PROJECT PLANNER

At the end of this unit, you will create a comic strip. Turn to page 114 of your SourceBook and read about that Project. Between now and the time you make your comic strip, keep a list of funny events that might give you inspiration for your comic strip. Look at comic strips in newspapers, and cut out some you think are really funny.

Answer the following questions to help you prepare for the Project.

1. Review "Mr. and Mrs. Juicy-O." Which funny scene do you think would make a good comic strip?

   _____

   _____

2. What scenes from other selections in the SourceBook would work in comic strip form?

   _____

   _____

   _____

3. In the Workshops for this unit, you wrote a fractured fairy tale and a funny poem. What were some of the things you did to make them funny?

   _____

   _____

   _____

4. How could you make your fractured fairy tale into a comic strip?

   _____

   _____

5. What tips about creating a comic strip did you learn from Robb Armstrong?

   _____

   _____

PUT YOUR IMAGINATION TO WORK

Complete the crossword puzzle with the words from the box.

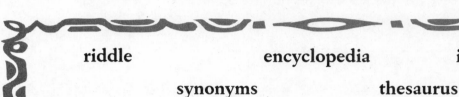

riddle   encyclopedia   imagination

synonyms   thesaurus

ACROSS

3. the ability to form pictures in the mind

5. a book or set of books containing information arranged alphabetically on many different subjects

DOWN

1. words that have similar meanings

2. a dictionary of synonyms

4. a question or problem that requires clever thinking to answer it

Design a library of the future. Use at least three words from the box.

Name _____

WINNING WITH RIDDLES

1. What made it so hard for Amy to be Peter's younger sister?

   _____

   _____

   _____

2. How is the way Amy succeeded in stumping Peter with riddles different from the way she'd planned?

   _____

   _____

   _____

3. How did Amy and Peter's relationship change after her success with riddles?

   _____

   _____

   _____

4. Mike Thaler talks about using synonyms to create riddles. Amy didn't use a synonym to make up her cake riddle. What kind of word play did she use?

   _____

   _____

   _____

HOW TO WRITE A HUMOROUS STORY

Write a humorous story in which riddles play a key role. Use the questions in the chart below to organize the ideas for your story.

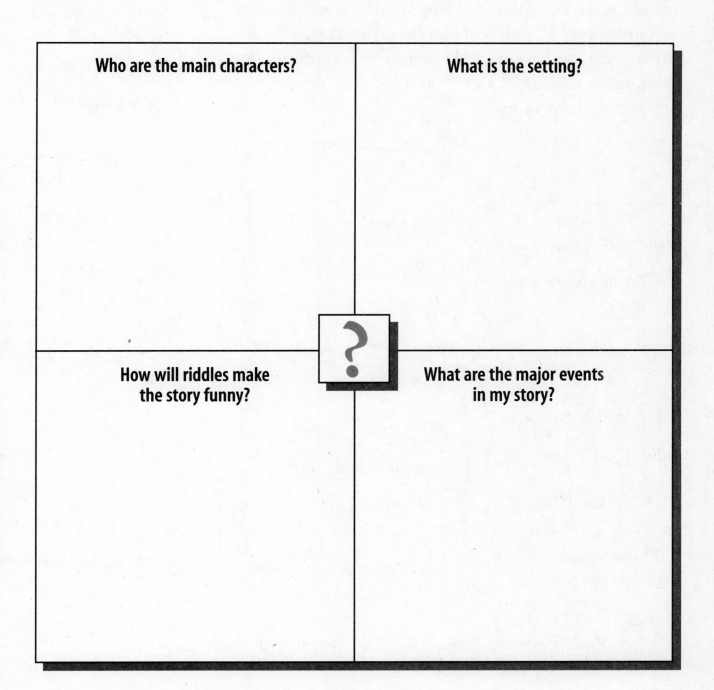

Who are the main characters?

What is the setting?

?

How will riddles make the story funny?

What are the major events in my story?

What riddles will I include in my story?
Who will ask and answer the riddles?
Can I build a story around riddles?

Name

KIDTALK REPORTS

You are the anchorperson for *Kidtalk,* a news show for children. You want to tell your viewers about Amy's success at riddles. Which information will you include in your report? Which will you leave out? Draw an *X* through the cue card with the unimportant information. Then, in each blank cue card, add another piece of important information.

Important information supports the main idea of the selection. Unimportant information does not.

Amy wanted to learn some riddles that her brother didn't know.

The book was under the librarian's desk.

It turned out that Peter had already read the book.

Amy finally stumped Peter by making up her own riddles.

Explain why the information you crossed out above is unimportant.

HORSEPLAY

by Jin Kee Shin

As you read the following scene from a novel, write your questions and ideas about it in the column on the right. Then complete page 58.

Maya loved horses, even though she had never ridden one. Her bedroom walls were covered with horse pictures. Horse books filled her bookshelves. She stared at her collection every night and sighed, "One day I'll get to ride a horse."

One morning, Maya saw an announcement in the newspaper. A local riding stable was holding a riddle contest. The person who wrote the best riddle about horses would win free riding lessons. Maya was determined to win. She made a list of horse words: *trot, canter, gallop.*

Next she started thinking up riddles. First she wrote, "How do horses send letters? Mare mail." Not good enough, she decided. Then she tried another: "Where do sick horses go? To the horse-pital." Not bad, she thought, but I can do better. Next she wrote, "Where do horses stay on their honeymoon? The bridle suite." She liked that one and was almost going to send it in when she had a brainstorm. She wrote it down and mailed it to the stable.

The contest winners were going to be announced on the radio. At last, the announcer came on. First he explained the contest. Then he read the two runner-up riddles. After that, he announced the winner's name—it was Maya! She was so excited that she almost forgot to listen when the announcer read her winning riddle. "Why did the pony lose its voice?" the announcer asked. He paused for just a second before giving the answer. "Because it was just a little horse!"

My questions and ideas as I read

IMPORTANT/UNIMPORTANT INFORMATION

Read "Horseplay" on page 57. Then write a postcard that Maya might write to her friend, Lee. Include the most important information in the story. Use the scrap paper below the postcard to note some of the unimportant information that you decided not to include.

Important information supports the main idea of the selection. Unimportant information does not.

Hi, Lee,

Bye for now, Maya

Lee Young

123 Main St.

Van Nuys, CA 91411

 Write another postcard from Maya, after her first riding lesson. Describe only the most important information about her lesson.

WHAT'S SO FUNNY?

What funny idea did you choose for your comic strip?
**On the lines below, tell what will happen in
your comic strip.**

_____

_____

_____

**Now plan your comic strip. For each panel,
make a rough sketch of the characters who
will appear, and write their dialogue in speech
balloons.**

PANEL 1: THE CHARACTERS	PANEL 2: SET UP THE JOKE

PANEL 3: ADD TO THE JOKE	PANEL 4: GIVE THE PUNCHLINE

MAKE IT FUNNIER

Look over the chart you filled in on page 59.
Is your cartoon as funny as you can make it?

**Answer the following questions to help
you make it better.**

1. Is the story you are telling in your cartoon clear?
   What would make it clearer?

   _____

   _____

2. Are the characters' words funny? What changes would make them funnier?

   _____

   _____

3. Do the characters' expressions match their words? What can you do to make
   them match better?

   _____

   _____

4. What should the background be for each panel? Is there a setting that would
   make your cartoon seem even funnier?

   _____

   _____

5. What other improvements would you like to make?

   _____

   _____

Use your answers to help you as you prepare the final version of your cartoon.

WHAT DID I LEARN?

1. What are the steps involved in making a cartoon strip?

_____

_____

_____

_____

2. What kinds of skills would it be important for a cartoonist to have?

_____

_____

_____

_____

3. What kinds of problems might you face as a professional cartoonist? How would you go about solving them?

_____

_____

_____

_____

4. On a separate sheet of paper, draw a picture or write about something you did in the Cartoonist's Studio.

BE A BETTER READER

Use the following questions to help you be a better reader.

☐ Do I try to make a picture in my mind while I read? Do I ask myself, "How do the characters look? How does the setting look?" Picturing what is happening can make a book come to life.

☐ Do I shift the speed as I read, depending on my purpose for reading and the type of book? Sometimes I want to read slowly and savor every word. Other times, I'm skimming for specific information.

☐ Do I make connections between what I read and my own life? Do I think about experiences I've had that are similar to what I'm reading about?

☐ Do I use what I know about the world, what sounds right, what I know about words, and the actual letters in a word to figure out what an unknown word means?

☐ Do I ask myself questions about what I'm reading? Do I keep on reading to answer my own questions?

WHY DO I NEED TO READ?	HOW CAN I BE A BETTER READER?	WHAT ADVANTAGE WILL IT GIVE ME?

READER'S LOG

Keep track of books you read about creative expression. When you've finished the unit, look over your list. Which book did you like best? Why?

Book Title	Author	Genre	Connection to Creative Expression

My favorite book: _____

Reasons why I like this book best: _____

_____

_____

_____

WORDS ENDING IN -y

1. Write the plural form of each word below. Remember that if a base word ends in a consonant and -y, change the y to i before you add -es.

bay _____   cry _____

body _____   diary _____

chimney _____   donkey _____

country _____   pony _____

2. Now circle the plural words you wrote, which are hidden in the puzzle. The words can go across, up, down, diagonally, and backward.

S	L	C	D	L	N	C	P	I
D	T	O	O	U	P	H	T	Q
B	O	U	P	O	N	I	E	S
O	Y	N	Z	W	E	M	D	E
D	S	T	K	S	P	N	D	I
I	E	R	E	E	S	E	I	R
E	I	I	W	M	Y	Y	E	A
S	R	E	B	A	Y	S	S	I
C	T	S	S	Y	A	R	F	D

3. For an added challenge, see how many other plural words you can find in the puzzle. Write them on another sheet of paper.

Make your own Find-a-Word puzzle. Use verbs ending in -y to which the suffix -ed has been added.

THE SCHWA SOUND

Many of the words in the puzzle have not one, but two schwa sounds. To complete the puzzle, choose the word from the box that matches each definition.

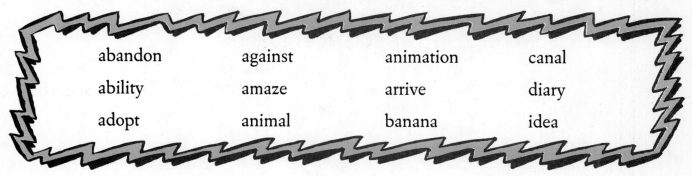

abandon	against	animation	canal
ability	amaze	arrive	diary
adopt	animal	banana	idea

ACROSS
2. A yellow fruit
4. Leave behind
5. Not in favor of
7. Movie made with cartoon characters
8. Record of personal experiences
10. To get someplace

DOWN
1. Narrow waterway
3. Make one's own
4. Skill
5. Fill with wonder
6. A living thing that is not a plant
9. A new thought

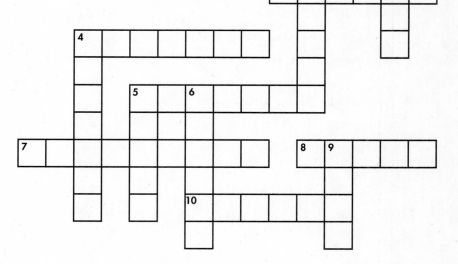

How many other words can you think of that have two schwa sounds? Use a dictionary to check each word you think of.

A CHARTFUL OF INFORMATION

Read the chart and answer each question below it. Fill in the
bubble beside the correct answer.

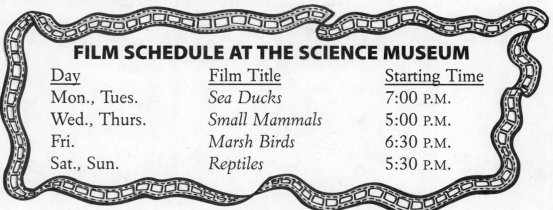

FILM SCHEDULE AT THE SCIENCE MUSEUM

Day	Film Title	Starting Time
Mon., Tues.	*Sea Ducks*	7:00 P.M.
Wed., Thurs.	*Small Mammals*	5:00 P.M.
Fri.	*Marsh Birds*	6:30 P.M.
Sat., Sun.	*Reptiles*	5:30 P.M.

1. What information can be found in the chart?
   - (a) when the science museum opens
   - (b) when the science films can be seen
   - (c) where ducks can be found

2. When is the film *Marsh Birds* being shown?
   - (a) Friday at 5:30 P.M.
   - (b) Wednesday at 5:00 P.M.
   - (c) Friday at 6:30 P.M.

3. What film is being shown on Sunday?
   - (a) *Marsh Birds*
   - (b) *Reptiles*
   - (c) *Sea Ducks*

4. How many of the films are shown twice a week?
   - (a) 1
   - (b) 3
   - (c) 4

Make a chart that shows the schedule of some of the TV programs you like to
watch. Use the headings "Name of Program," "Day," and "Starting Time."

Name

WORDS WITH /s/

The clues below define words with /s/, which may be spelled *s*, *ss*, *sc*, and *c*. Complete puzzle A and puzzle B. Then read the letters running down the shaded column. You will discover two words that contain the four different spellings of /s/.

A

1. the warmest season of the year
2. frozen water
3. smooth, shiny fabric
4. opposite of more
5. large body of water
6. the sound made by speaking
7. for sure; without doubt
8. school subject

B

1. an animal that can race
2. to choose
3. a show with clowns and acrobats
4. a picture or a place
5. a drink with bubbles
6. to keep for later

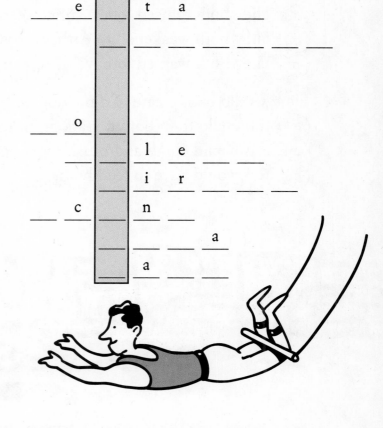

In the word *science*, /s/ is spelled two different ways. Work with a partner to think of other words that use more than one way to spell /s/. Check your words in a dictionary, if you wish.

ALIKE OR DIFFERENT?

Fill in the bubble beside the best answer.

1. Which sentence best compares what Arthur and his Poppa wanted for Thanksgiving dinner?
   - (a) They both agreed that turkey would be best.
   - (b) Poppa wanted turkey and Arthur wanted chicken.
   - (c) Poppa wanted turkey and Arthur preferred pizza.

2. Which sentence is true about Arthur and his pet chicken?
   - (a) Arthur weighed more than his pet chicken.
   - (b) His pet chicken was taller and heavier than Arthur.
   - (c) His pet chicken was the same age as Arthur.

3. In what way were Momma and Poppa alike?
   - (a) They both refused to let Arthur keep the chicken.
   - (b) They both weakened to Arthur's wish to keep the chicken.
   - (c) They both wanted to have the chicken for dinner.

4. How would taking care of a pet dog be like taking care of a pet chicken?
   - (a) You could train both to bark at intruders.
   - (b) You would comb and brush them both.
   - (c) You would have to feed both.

Summarize the excerpt of *The Hoboken Chicken Emergency* for two different people. Compare how they react. Write some words under each person's name that describes how he or she reacted.

Name

ADDING PREFIXES AND SUFFIXES

A. A prefix comes at the beginning of a word and changes the meaning of the word. For instance, *reopen* means "to open again," and *unfriendly* means "not friendly." On each line, write the word from the box that goes with the definition.

restart	recycle	unhappy	unlike	review	unwise

1. not smart

_____

2. to look back at

_____

3. to use again

_____

4. sad

_____

5. to begin again

_____

6. different

_____

B. A suffix comes at the end of a word. Unscramble each jumbled word below, and write it in the box. Then, write the base word without the suffix.

1. nikhig

base word _____

2. vilgin

base word _____

3. gasniv

base word _____

4. ligfyn

base word _____

Now unscramble the circled letters to answer the riddle:

What was the laundry doing? Just _____ out!

 Make up clues for words with the prefixes *un-* and *re-* and the suffixes *-ed, -er,* and *-ing.* Give them to a classmate to solve.

Name

THE SOUND OF IT

Write a homophone for the underlined word. Then fill in the bubble next to the sentence in which the homophone you wrote would make sense.

1. "Sally's the <u>whole</u> steamboat," he said.

   _____

   (a) Who has gobbled up the _____ pumpkin pie?
   (b) He drilled a _____ right through the sheet of ice.
   (c) It took the _____ day to reach the mountain top.

2. Sally can whip across the river, using her apron for a <u>sail</u>.

   _____

   (a) He bought that old broken toaster at a yard _____ .
   (b) The red and white _____ flapped in the wind.
   (c) The big ship will set _____ at the crack of dawn.

Fill in the bubble beside the sentence with a homograph for the underlined word.

3. Sally can laugh the <u>bark</u> off a pine tree.
   (a) The beaver used strips of bark to build its house.
   (b) The woodpecker tapped away at the bark for hours.
   (c) A loud bark woke up the whole neighborhood.

4. Her anger <u>rose</u> higher than a Mississippi flood.
   (a) At high tide the ocean rose up to the dunes.
   (b) She carefully placed the rose in a tall thin vase.
   (c) The kite rose quickly with the next gust of wind.

Look for other homophones and homographs in "Sally Ann Thunder Ann Whirlwind." Write pairs of sentences for as many as you can.

LOOKING FOR WORDS

Fill in the bubble beside the best answer to each question.

1. Where would you find the meaning of the word *fantasy?*
   - (a) in a dictionary
   - (b) in a thesaurus

2. Where would you find a choice of synonyms for the word *communicate?*
   - (a) in a dictionary
   - (b) in a thesaurus

3. Where is the best place to find an antonym for the word *humorous?*
   - (a) in a dictionary
   - (b) in a thesaurus

4. Where would you find out how to pronounce the word *whimsical?*
   - (a) in a dictionary
   - (b) in a thesaurus

5. Where would you find a more precise word for the word *interesting?*
   - (a) in a dictionary
   - (b) in a thesaurus

 Use the word *amusing* in a sentence to describe something you saw, read, or heard. Then check a thesaurus to find synonyms for *amusing*. Make up several sentences using the synonyms.

Name

COMPOUND WORDS

Complete the sentences below using open, closed, or hyphenated compound words. Form each compound with one word from each box. The first one has been done for you.

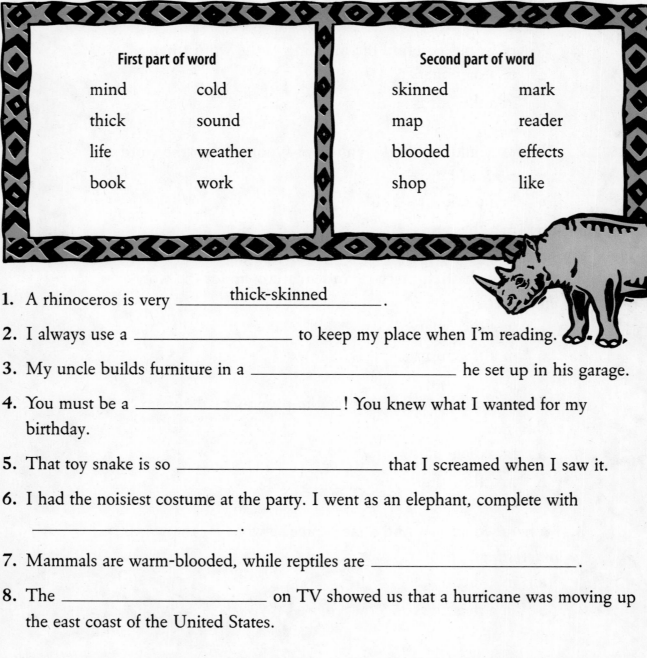

First part of word		Second part of word	
mind	cold	skinned	mark
thick	sound	map	reader
life	weather	blooded	effects
book	work	shop	like

1. A rhinoceros is very ___thick-skinned___.

2. I always use a _____ to keep my place when I'm reading.

3. My uncle builds furniture in a _____ he set up in his garage.

4. You must be a _____! You knew what I wanted for my birthday.

5. That toy snake is so _____ that I screamed when I saw it.

6. I had the noisiest costume at the party. I went as an elephant, complete with _____.

7. Mammals are warm-blooded, while reptiles are _____.

8. The _____ on TV showed us that a hurricane was moving up the east coast of the United States.

Make a game of Concentration with a small group of classmates. Write each half of a compound word on an index card. Make your game challenging by including open, closed, and hyphenated compound words.

Name

ORDER, PLEASE!

The groups of sentences below tell about Lane Smith. They are not listed in the order in which they happened.

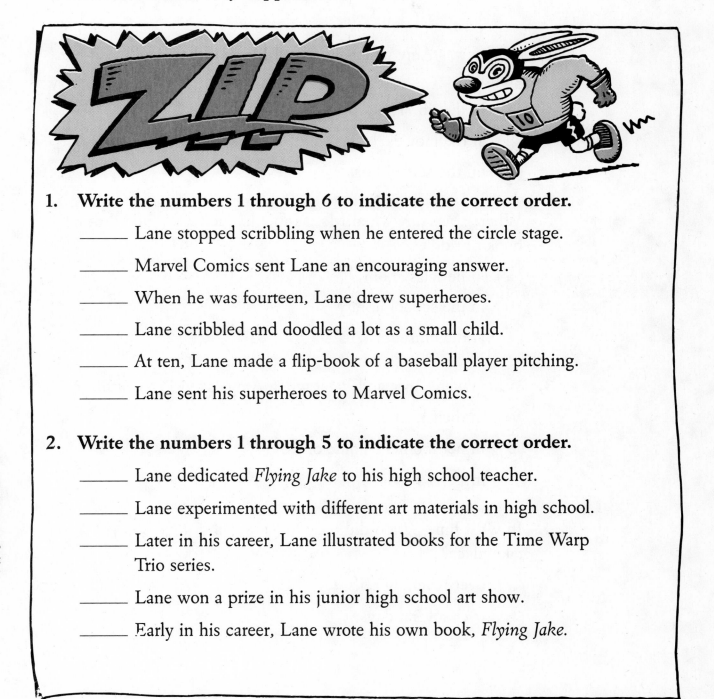

1. **Write the numbers 1 through 6 to indicate the correct order.**

    _____ Lane stopped scribbling when he entered the circle stage.

    _____ Marvel Comics sent Lane an encouraging answer.

    _____ When he was fourteen, Lane drew superheroes.

    _____ Lane scribbled and doodled a lot as a small child.

    _____ At ten, Lane made a flip-book of a baseball player pitching.

    _____ Lane sent his superheroes to Marvel Comics.

2. **Write the numbers 1 through 5 to indicate the correct order.**

    _____ Lane dedicated *Flying Jake* to his high school teacher.

    _____ Lane experimented with different art materials in high school.

    _____ Later in his career, Lane illustrated books for the Time Warp Trio series.

    _____ Lane won a prize in his junior high school art show.

    _____ Early in his career, Lane wrote his own book, *Flying Jake*.

 THINK & WRITE Write five sentences about events that happened in school this year. Number the events from 1 to 5 to show the order in which they happened.

Name

WHERE'S IT HAPPENING?

The following questions are about *The Riddle Streak.* Fill in the bubble beside the best answer.

1. Where was Amy when she asked Maria if they could visit her grandfather?
   - (a) in the library
   - (b) at the movies
   - (c) on the school bus

2. Where was Amy when Ms. Morris handed her a brand-new book of riddles?
   - (a) in her classroom
   - (b) in the school library
   - (c) at the museum

3. Where were Amy and Peter when Amy asked Peter riddles?
   - (a) in their kitchen
   - (b) in her mother's home office
   - (c) in Peter's room

4. In what time period did the events in *The Riddle Streak* take place?
   - (a) over several weeks
   - (b) over several days
   - (c) in one day

Think of one of your favorite stories. Make a list of all the places where the story events happen.

WHAT'S THE PROBLEM?

Fill in the bubble beside the best answer to each question about
The Riddle Streak.

1. Which sentence best describes the story problem?
- (a) Amy had to write some riddles for school.
- (b) Amy wanted to beat her older brother at something.
- (c) Amy could not find a good riddle book.

2. What is one of the steps Amy took to solve her problem?
- (a) Amy read every riddle book in the library.
- (b) Amy looked in the dictionary for riddles.
- (c) Amy copied riddles from a new riddle book.

3. What is another step that Amy took to solve her problem?
- (a) Amy made up riddles of her own.
- (b) Amy asked her mother to help her make up riddles.
- (c) Amy helped her mother mix cake batter.

4. Which sentence best describes the outcome of the story?
- (a) Peter answered all of Amy's riddles.
- (b) Amy gave up trying to do better than Peter at something.
- (c) Amy successfully stumped Peter with her riddles.

Think of a movie you liked. Make a chart that shows what problem the main character faced, what he or she did to try to solve it, and the outcome.

LISTENER'S GUIDE

Use this guide to record what you hear.

Title of Selection: _____

Author: _____

How I felt about the story: _____

_____

_____

_____

My favorite part: _____

_____

_____

_____

My least favorite part: _____

_____

_____

_____

Would you recommend that a friend listen to this story? Explain.

_____

_____

_____

_____

LITERACY-at-WORK
BOOK

UNIT 5

NATURE GUIDES

SEA OTTER

MANAGING INFORMATION

TABLE OF CONTENTS

NATURE GUIDES

★ NEWSLETTER ★

WELCOME TO *NATURE GUIDES!*

Step outside. Notice the plants and animals in your neighborhood. Whether you live in the country, the suburbs, or the city, there's an amazing natural world to discover. In this book you'll meet and read about people who observe, study, and enjoy nature.

What does this unit have in store for you? Take a look at what your *Nature Guides* SourceBook has to offer. You'll be a nature expert soon.

Nature Notes

Jean Craighead George is famous for her environmental fiction stories. In this section you'll learn all about alligators as you read a story by her. Then you'll read about a kid named Ali Baba. See how a rumor turns into a bear of a story.

+PLUS+ Discover more fascinating facts about alligators in a children's encyclopedia article.

WILD THINGS

Lions and tigers and bears—oh, my! You won't find these animals in this section. But you will meet a girl who swims with sea lions—really! Then you'll read several Native American legends about the sections—or moons—on a turtle's back.

+PLUS+

Read an African folk tale that explains how the leopard got its spots.

Let's Meet Veronica Gonzales-Vest

She can point out a tiny flower from 50 yards. She can close her eyes and tell you what birds are singing. And she can tell you how to stay safe from bears. She's Veronica Gonzales-Vest, and she's a park ranger who really is queen of the mountains!

★ NEWSLETTER ★

Take a Hike!

First you'll read an urban field guide and discover that there are more plants and animals in your backyard than you would think. Then you'll take a walk with a naturalist, Jim Arnosky, as he tells how he observes nature.

+PLUS+ Observe a boy who spends his summer vacation watching a mysterious black fox.

Let's Visit a National Park Headquarters

Whether you're going for a swim, a hike, or an overnight camping trip, the national parks are the place to be. But before you leave, check out the park headquarters. It's a cool place—packed with important information to keep you safe and make sure you have fun.

THINGS YOU'LL DO

How well can you observe nature? Look, listen, and then write in your own *nature log*. Find an interesting plant or animal, and then study it. Share what you've learned with others as you draw a *wildlife diagram*. Now that your head is bursting with nature information, you can create your own *field guide*.

Getting Started

Ready to take a walk in the forest? You don't have to go very far to start seeing nature at work. Unscramble these forest words to see what's waiting for you.

velesa _____
erets _____
mnkupchi _____
reabs _____
low _____
lerrsiuqs _____
eagrdn ksnea _____

Answers: leaves, trees, chipmunk, bears, owl, squirrels, garden snake

WELCOME TO NATIONAL PARK HEADQUARTERS

1. What do you think a national park is?

    _____

    _____

    _____

    _____

2. What do you think a park ranger does?

    _____

    _____

    _____

    _____

3. What do you want to know about national parks?

    _____

    _____

    _____

    _____

4. How could you find out more about national parks?

    _____

    _____

    _____

    _____

STUDENT LOG

Here's a way to keep track of what you do in the National Park Headquarters.
Fill in the chart when you visit the National Park Headquarters.

Date	Time I Spent	What I Did	What I Learned

REPTILES GALORE!

Read the article below. Write the correct word from the box in each blank.

alligator:	a large reptile with a long tail and thick skin
cypress:	a kind of evergreen tree with small needles and woody cones
egret:	a kind of heron with white feathers
saw grass:	a kind of plant with grasslike, sharp-spined leaves
algae:	simple plant life that lives in water
rookery:	a breeding place or colony of birds
endangered:	threatened with extinction
sanctuaries:	safe, protected places for wildlife where hunting is illegal

STATE OPENS SWAMP HABITAT

The state has opened a new swamp habitat that contains swamp creatures, such as the long-tailed (1) _____ and other reptiles. A white-feathered (2) _____ can be seen among the small needles and woody cones of the (3) _____ tree. The habitat also has (4) _____, or safe places, for (5) _____ animals—animals at risk of becoming extinct. Among these safe places is a (6) _____ , where rare birds breed. Elsewhere, signs caution visitors about (7) _____ . Its sharp jagged leaves protrude from the water. (8) _____ , simple forms of plant life that live in the water, have turned the water greenish-brown.

Make a map of a swamp habitat like the one described above. Label the map with at least four words from the box.

A 'GATOR TALE

Your teacher has asked you to give a report on alligators. Using what you've learned from *The Moon of the Alligators* and "Alligators," fill in the index cards below to help prepare for your report.

The American alligator can be found:

_____

_____

_____

_____

One difference between alligators and crocodiles is:

_____

_____

_____

_____

Congress has helped the alligator by:

_____

_____

_____

_____

Two reasons why alligators almost died out are:

_____

_____

_____

_____

One way alligators attract their prey is:

_____

_____

_____

_____

FICTION: POINT OF VIEW

Write a story describing the daily life of an animal. Choose an animal. Write your story from this animal's point of view. Fill in the chart below to help you.

Animal: _____

Facts about where the animal lives: _____

_____

What the animal eats: _____

_____

What the animal does: _____

_____

_____

Feelings the animal has about its surroundings: _____

_____

_____

What happens to the animal: _____

_____

_____

_____

_____

Do I know enough about my animal to write about its life?
Can I write from the animal's point of view?
Can I imagine how the animal feels?

Name

ALLIGATOR EYES

Complete the chain below to tell about what happened in *The Moon of the Alligators*. On each blank line, fill in what happened as a result of the thing that came before.

When you read, ask yourself, What changes have taken place in the story? Why did the changes happen? What effect have they had?

CAUSE/EFFECT CHAIN

The alligator was hungry.

_____

Because of this . . .

_____

Because of this . . .

_____

Because of this . . .

_____

Because of this . . .

_____

Because of this . . .

_____

What might have happened if Congress hadn't made the alligator an endangered species? In a sentence or two, tell what effect this might have had on the alligator of Sawgrass Hole.

WHY ARE THE RAIN FORESTS DISAPPEARING?

from Banners: *Save the Earth*

As you read the story, write your questions and ideas about it in the column on the right. Then complete page 10.

Most rain forests are located in countries where much of the population is poor. Many of these people have little money for food. Many are encouraged by their governments to leave their overcrowded cities and move to the rain forests.

Some members of the governments of these countries see rain forests as places to be cleared for farming. This causes a problem. Why? After a few years, the cleared land can no longer grow food. So the people, known as slash-and-burn farmers, must move further into the forests, cutting and burning as they go.

People who have always called the rain forest home are also caught in a two-way bind. They depend on the rain forest for much-needed food and shelter, but they also need to cut down trees for fuel and firewood.

Loggers also contribute to the crisis. In order to earn their living, they must cut down trees to build houses and furniture. The hard-to-get wood is shipped to the United States and other wealthy nations.

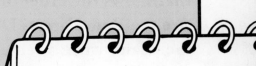

My questions and ideas as I read

CAUSE/EFFECT

The boxes below are for making a cause/effect chain that shows the order of events in "Why Are the Rain Forests Disappearing?" To create the chain, write a sentence in each box that shows how one event led to another.

A cause is the reason something happens. An effect is what results from a cause. Sometimes one effect becomes the cause of another effect.

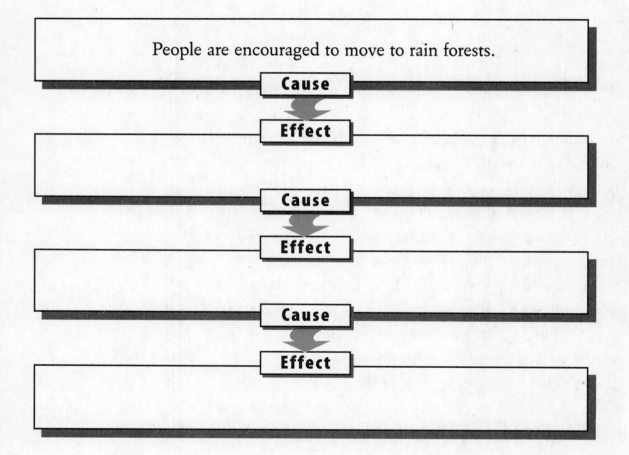

People are encouraged to move to rain forests.

Cause

Effect

Cause

Effect

Cause

Effect

THINK & WRITE Make a list of things you can do to save the rain forests and to help the people who live there.

Name

PARTS OF A WHOLE

The compound words in the first column are from *The Moon of the Alligators*. Your job is to complete the chart by writing the two words that make up the compound word. Then write the meaning of the word. In the last column, tell whether the word is written as one word, two words, or a hyphenated word.

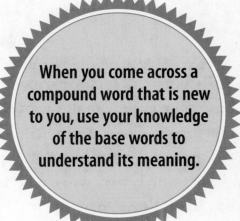

When you come across a compound word that is new to you, use your knowledge of the base words to understand its meaning.

COMPOUND WORD	BASE WORD	BASE WORD	MEANING OF COMPOUND WORD	WHAT KIND?
man-made				
homeland				
alligator holes				
limestone				
soft-shelled				

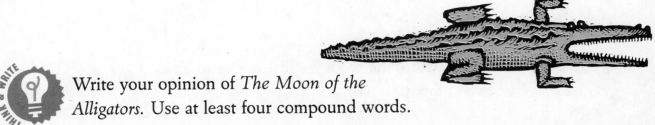

THINK & WRITE Write your opinion of *The Moon of the Alligators*. Use at least four compound words.

COMPOUND WORDS

The chart shows compound words from "Why Are the Rain Forests Disappearing?" on page 9. Write the two base words that make up each compound and their meanings. Then define the compound word. In the last column, tell what type of compound word the word is —one word, two words, or hyphenated. The first one has been done for you.

> To understand a compound word, separate it into its base words. Combining the meanings of base words often explains compound words.

COMPOUND WORD	BASE WORD	BASE WORD	MEANING OF COMPOUND WORD	WHAT KIND?
rain forest	rain: Precipitation	forest: tree-covered	tree-covered land with a lot of precipitation	*two* words
overcrowded				
two-way				
firewood				
much-needed				

Write a paragraph describing what it's like to live in a rain forest. Use at least two compound words.

Copyright © 1996 Scholastic Inc.

PLAN A ROUTE TO YELLOWSTONE

The nation's oldest national park is beautiful — and so are many other national parks! Look at the map below. Then plan a route from your home to Yellowstone that includes stops at a few other parks. If you live in Alaska or Hawaii, think of where your plane will land and draw your route from there.

NATIONAL PARK HEADQUARTERS

Mark your town on the map with a star. Then draw the route from your home to Yellowstone and back. You don't have to travel the same route twice.

Why did you choose these routes? _____

_____

What kind of transportation will you use? _____

_____

How many states will you travel through? _____

_____

WILDLIFE IN A PARK

Read the words and their definitions. Then write the word from the box that fits each clue.

national park: land preserved by the federal government for the public to visit

wildlife: wild plants and animals in their natural surroundings

park ranger: a person who takes care of a park

site: the place where something is located

sequoia: a very tall evergreen tree with large cones that grows in California

1. This tree grows in California and has pine cones. It is a

   _____ .

2. A word that sounds just like *sight* but refers to a place is

   _____ .

3. The government set aside land so that people could visit

   the _____ at Yosemite.

4. A person who works in Grand Teton, Yellowstone, or Yosemite

   teaching the public about the area is a _____ .

5. Moose, buffalo, and deer that live in their natural

   environment are examples of _____ .

You are a park ranger. Use at least four words from the box to write a diary entry that tells about your day.

WHERE'S THE BEAR?

Use what you learned from "Ali Baba Hunts for a Bear" and from the interview with Veronica Gonzales-Vest to answer the following questions.

1. What two fun activities did Ali Baba enjoy in the national park?

_____

_____

_____

2. If Ali Baba asked Veronica Gonzales-Vest how she knew the ages of the sequoia trees, what would her response be?

_____

_____

_____

3. What happened when Ali Baba accidentally told a lie about seeing a bear? What effect did his lie have on others?

_____

_____

_____

4. What tips would Veronica Gonzales-Vest give about observing wildlife?

_____

_____

_____

WHERE THERE ARE WILD THINGS

One of Veronica Gonzales-Vest's jobs is to tell park visitors about plants and animals that live in Sequoia National Park. Now you are a national park ranger, too.

Choose a park animal or plant that interests you and prepare a short talk about it. Then present your talk to your classmates.

You can use the space below for notes.

Name of plant or animal:

_____

Where to see it:

_____

Description:

_____

Fascinating facts:

Now you're ready to give your nature talk. When you begin, remember to introduce yourself. Be sure to look at your audience and smile. And, like park ranger Veronica Gonzales-Vest, be sure to put lots of enthusiasm in your voice. Share your love of nature with the "park visitors" in your classroom.

FICTION: PLOT

Write a brief story in which a misunderstanding leads to
a surprising twist in the plot. Use the chart to help you.

The misunderstanding:

The main character:

What happens in the story:

The surprising twist:

The ending:

Is the plot clear?

Will readers understand the order of events?

Is there a misunderstanding that causes a surprising twist in the plot?

Name

GET THE POINT!

For each purpose, write one detail from "Ali Baba Hunts for a Bear" to show that the author had this purpose in mind. Then answer the question in the box on the right.

Try to figure out why the author included specific details. This can help you evaluate the author's purpose, which can be to inform, to persuade, or to entertain.

Author's Purpose: To Inform
Detail:

Author's Purpose: To Entertain
Detail:

Author's Purpose: To Persuade
Detail:

Which purpose do you think is most important? Support your argument with details.

Copyright © 1996 Scholastic Inc.

How would "Ali Baba Hunts for a Bear" be different if the author's only purpose was to inform?

Name

A DOG'S LIFE

By Meish Goldish
Read the story. Then use it to complete page 20.

"Nothing is going right today," said Al. He scowled as he entered the room. "The world is going to the dogs!"

"Well, don't blame the dogs," said Sharon. "They happen to be great creatures."

"Says you," snapped Al. "Once I had a dog, and all it did was bark. The world doesn't need dogs."

"You are doggone silly!" Sharon replied. "The world certainly *does* need dogs!"

"For what?" Al challenged.

"For plenty," Sharon said. "First, dogs make good companions. My grandmother lives alone, and her dog keeps her company."

"Okay, so maybe a few lonely people need dogs, but that's all," Al argued.

"That's *not* all," Sharon said. "The police use dogs to track down criminals and locate missing persons. And blind people have seeing-eye dogs to guide them. People also use dogs to guard their homes and businesses."

"That's true," Al admitted.

"And don't forget dogs that herd sheep," Sharon added.

"I guess," Al mumbled softly.

"And," Sharon said, "I haven't mentioned the most important reason we need dogs. They make great pets!"

"What you say may be true," Al admitted. "But if you think you'll convince me to get a pet dog, you're barking up the wrong tree!"

"You may change your mind some day," Sharon said. "All it will take is puppy love!"

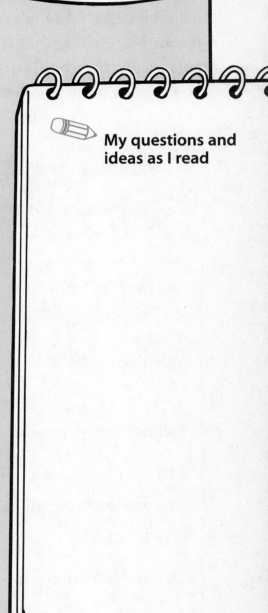

My questions and ideas as I read

EVALUATE AUTHOR'S PURPOSE

After you read "A Dog's Life," look at the details
the author includes in the story. Decide which
details inform, which persuade, and which entertain.
Write them under the proper headings below. Then
tell how the details fulfill the author's purpose.

When you read, try
to figure out why the
author included certain
details. This will help
you evaluate the
author's purpose.

Details that inform:

What does the author want you to learn?

Details that persuade:

What does the author want you to believe?

Details that entertain:

How does the author entertain you?

Think of an animal you would like to write a story about. What would your
purpose be in writing the story? List the details you would use in the story.

PUT IT IN CONTEXT

**Complete the chart. Use context clues to
figure out the meaning of the underlined words.**

Study the
context clues, or the
words that surround an
unfamiliar word, to
figure out what
it means.

Unfamiliar Word in Context	Context Clues or Reason	Meaning of Unfamiliar Word
"Ali Baba spent all his time searching for a bear....Mr. Bernstein grabbed his camera, ready to focus it at the <u>elusive</u> animal."		
"So Ali Baba spent the next hour concentrating on riding and not on bears.... He couldn't wait to go home and brag to Robert about his newest <u>accomplishment</u>."		

THINK & WRITE

Write a paragraph about looking for a bear. Include
a nonsense word and context clues for it. Ask a
partner to figure out the meaning of the word.

Name

CONTEXT CLUES: UNFAMILIAR WORDS

For each word below, write a sentence with context clues from "A Dog's Life" on page 19. Then define the word, and use it in a sentence of your own.

Look at the context clues, or the words that surround an unfamiliar word, to figure out what it means.

1. scowled

Sentence with context clues: _____

_____

Meaning of <u>scowled</u>: _____

Your sentence: _____

_____

2. companions

Sentence with context clues: _____

_____

Meaning of <u>companions</u>: _____

Your sentence: _____

_____

Find an unfamiliar word in your glossary, a dictionary, or something you read. Find out what the word means. Then use the word in a paragraph. Include at least two context clues.

IDENTIFY MYSTERY TRACKS

Park rangers find animal tracks all the time. What animals made the tracks below? Read the clues, then guess the animals.

NATIONAL PARK HEADQUARTERS

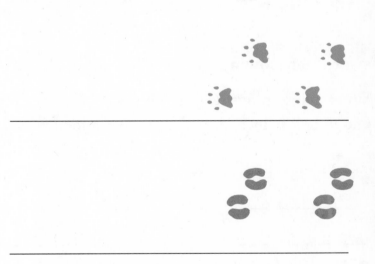

Yellowstone National Park is home to about 200 of these animals. They have thick fur and long claws.

_____

This animal is covered with long, sharp quills everywhere but on its belly. Watch out for it in Yosemite National Park!

_____

This animal is sometimes called a wildcat. Its spotted coat helps it hide among large rocks and trees at Yosemite National Park.

_____

One hundred years ago this huge, shaggy mammal was almost extinct. Today its numbers are on the rise in Yellowstone.

_____

What other animal tracks do you know? Draw and label a set of animal tracks in the space below. Use an encyclopedia or animal book if you need some ideas.

NATURE LOG

The scene below shows a variety of plants and animals that you might see in the desert in the southwestern United States.

Observe the picture carefully.

Answer the following questions:

1. What living things do you see in the picture? List as many as you can. If you don't know their names, describe them in a few words.

   _____

   _____

   _____

2. Pick one animal and one plant in the picture that interest you. Look at each one carefully and then describe it. Write as many details as you can.

   _____

   _____

   _____

OBSERVATIONS

Look back at the picture of the desert on page 24. Imagine that you are a scientist observing this scene. You will undoubtedly have questions about the living things you see.

1. Write two questions about the animals in this environment.

_____

_____

_____

_____

2. Write two questions about the plants in this environment.

_____

_____

_____

_____

3. What resources could you use to find out more about the animals and plants of the desert?

_____

_____

_____

_____

DOING RESEARCH

Read the following encyclopedia article.

AMPHIBIANS

Amphibian is the name of a class of vertebrates (animals with backbones). Amphibians spend part of their lives on land and part in water.

PHYSICAL FEATURES

Size   The smallest amphibians are tiny frogs 1/2 inch (1 cm) long. The largest are Japanese giant salamanders that can grow to a length of 5 feet (1.5 m). Most amphibians are no longer than 6 inches (15 cm).

Body Temperature   Amphibians are cold-blooded; that is, their body temperature matches that of their surroundings. They must avoid extremes of temperature to survive. Those that live in cool climates hibernate during the winter.

Skin   Amphibians have no hair, feathers, or scales. Most have smooth skin protected by a thick, damp coat of mucus. Mucus keeps the skin from drying out. Some toads have dry, leathery skin.

Breathing   Most adult amphibians live on land and have lungs that take in oxygen. Young amphibians and a few adults live in the water and breathe with gills.

KINDS OF AMPHIBIANS

Frogs and Toads   These are the most common amphibians. They have long hind legs that help them jump. Adults do not have tails. Most frogs and toads live in the tropics, but two kinds are found as far north as the Arctic Circle.

Salamanders   With their four legs and long bodies and tails, these animals look like lizards. A few species have only two legs. Most inhabit the temperate climate zones.

Caecilians   Caecilians make up the smallest group of amphibians. They resemble large worms and live in burrows under the earth. Some do not have eyes.

See also Animals, Frogs, Salamanders, and Toads.

1. What are the two main sections of the article?

_____

2. Which physical characteristics of amphibians are discussed?

_____

3. Where in this article would you look to find out how salamanders are different from frogs?

_____

4. Where else in the encyclopedia might you look to find out how salamanders are different from frogs?

_____

COME JOIN OUR JOURNEY!

Use the words from the box to complete the paragraph.

scuba dive: to swim underwater wearing scuba gear

research: close and careful study of a subject

snorkel: to swim underwater using a mask and a tube that allows breathing

naturalist: a person who studies plants and animals

voyage: a long journey made on a ship

expedition: a long trip made for a specific purpose, such as exploration or research

hammerhead: a kind of shark that has a hammer-shaped head

Sail to Adventure

Join our (1) _____ to explore and research the Hawaiian

Islands. Choose the subject on which you would like to do

(2) _____. Like a professional (3) _____,

you can study marine plant life. After you (4) _____

just below the water's surface, you'll want to use scuba gear to

(5) _____ to the sea floor. You may even see a

(6) _____ shark. Our luxury ships ensure that your

long trip will be a pleasant (7)_____.

Write a paragraph describing the kind of expedition a naturalist might go on. Use three words from the box.

VISIT THE GALÁPAGOS!

The girl from *Swimming With Sea Lions* is writing a travel guide to the Galápagos Islands. Help her complete the guide so that others will enjoy their trip as much as she did.

The Galápagos Islands are a great place to visit. *Galápagos* means (1)"_____" in old Spanish. The best way to see the Galápagos is by (2) _____ . That way you can jump off and go (3) _____ . One big creature you can see in the water is the (4) _____ . In the water, they (5) _____ _____ . They chase each other around and act like big kittens. A big creature you can see on land is (6) _____ . One sad part of the history of these creatures is that long ago, sailors came to the islands and (7) _____ . Another is that rats from the ships swam ashore and destroyed tortoise eggs and young tortoises. But the good news is that, thanks to (8) _____ and _____ , a lot of tortoises are being saved. One thing they are doing is (9) _____ at the station and eventually returning them to their own islands. One last thing: watch out for the (10) _____ . They sting!

Copyright © 1996 Scholastic Inc.

DIARY ENTRY

Write a diary entry about an experience you've had. Choose one you want to share with your classmates. Use the chart to help you.

The experience:

When and where it took place:

What happened:

My thoughts and feelings:

Descriptive details:

Have I chosen an experience that happened to me?

Have I included my thoughts and feelings?

Will my descriptions help readers picture the scenes?

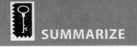
Name

LIGHTS, CAMERA, GALÁPAGOS!

Swimming With Sea Lions is being made into a movie. You need to give the director a summary of the story events of the first two days. In the space below, write your notes summarizing the most important points of those two days.

When you summarize, include a topic sentence and a few supporting sentences.

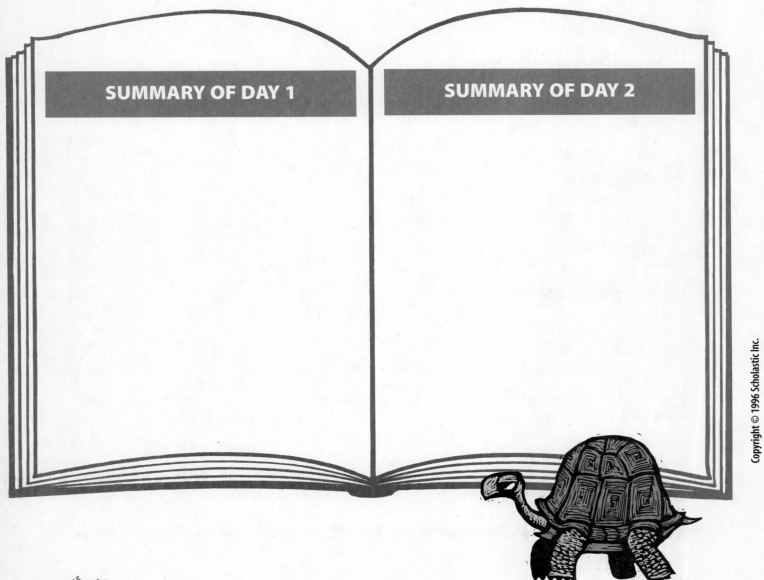

SUMMARY OF DAY 1

SUMMARY OF DAY 2

THINK & WRITE

You have just one day to spend on the Galápagos Islands. Use what you read in *Swimming With Sea Lions* to write a summary of what you would like to do.

MY DAYS AS A BUG WATCHER

By Chris Ramos
Read the selection. Then use it to complete page 32.

 My questions and ideas as I read

Day One

Dear Diary,

I've decided to study bugs. Actually, Aunt Bert suggested it last night, when we were sitting on the porch. My first project is to find out why insects fly around lights at night.

Day Two

Dear Diary,

I found my answer in a library book. When there are no electric lights, insects set their course by the moon. If they fly in a straight line, the moon is always in the same place. If they see an electric light, they fly around it to keep the light in the same place.

I tried an experiment from the book. I went down the driveway to the street. As I walked, the moon was always in front and to the right of me. But the street lamp kept changing position. The only way to keep the lamp in the same position was to walk around it.

Day Three

Dear Diary,

The book I read also told how to see like a bee. I tried that today. I took a magnifying glass and looked at the corner of a TV screen when the TV was on. I saw lots of little dots. This is what a bee sees when it looks at me.

SUMMARIZE

Read "My Days as a Bug Watcher."
Then complete the summaries
for Day One, Day Two, and
Day Three.

When you summarize, keep it short. Mention only the most important points.

On Day One, the writer decided to

On Day Two, the writer learned that

On Day Three, the writer looked at

 Choose a TV documentary you've seen or a book you've read about animals. Write a brief summary of it.

MAKE A WORDLESS SIGN

Many signs use symbols to get a message across without words. Create a sign showing a new symbol for a national park activity. When you're finished, see if a friend can figure out what your sign means!

NATIONAL PARK HEADQUARTERS

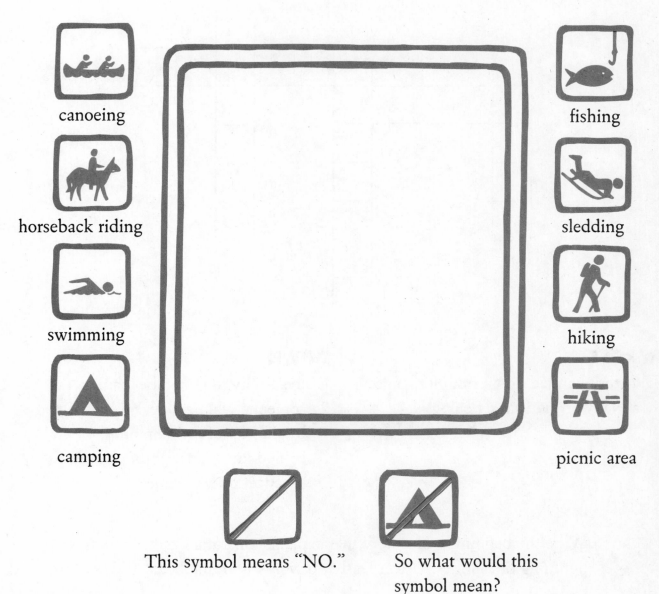

canoeing

horseback riding

swimming

camping

fishing

sledding

hiking

picnic area

This symbol means "NO."

So what would this symbol mean?

LEGENDARY WORDS

Complete the crossword puzzle with the words from the box that fit the clues.

lodge   memory   legend   elder   learned

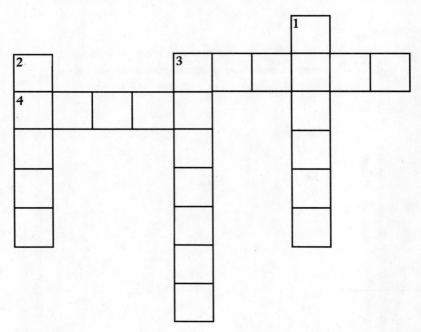

ACROSS

3. a story handed down from long ago

4. a Native American dwelling

DOWN

1. the ability to remember things

2. someone who is older and respected by the rest of the community

3. gained knowledge through study, practice, or experience

Write the beginning of a story that explains a natural event, such as lightning or thunder. Use at least two words from the box.

TELL ME WHY

1. In *Moon of Popping Trees,* what do the children know?

   _____

   _____

2. How did the people in "Budding Moon" solve their problem?

   _____

   _____

   _____

3. How did the Little People help the boy in the poem "Strawberry Moon"?
   How did the boy help the people of his village?

   _____

   _____

   _____

4. According to "Moon of Falling Leaves," why do the leaves fall off the
   trees each autumn?

   _____

   _____

5. What purpose do the poems in *Thirteen Moons on Turtle's Back* and
   the story "Leopard" both have?

   _____

   _____

   _____

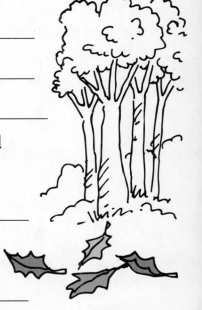

LEGEND

Play the role of a storyteller living long ago. Write a legend about a wonder in the natural world. Use the chart to help you.

The natural wonder my legend explains:

Larger-than-life characters:

Unusual events:

Descriptive details:

Will my legend explain a natural wonder?
Can I use larger-than-life characters and unusual events?

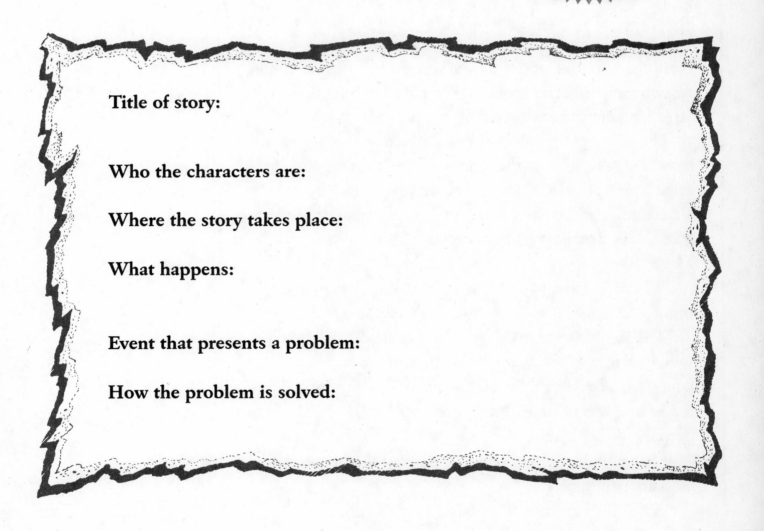
PLOTTING A STORY

Write a plot summary for either
"Moon of Popping Trees," "Strawberry Moon,"
or "Moon of Falling Leaves."
Fill out the chart below.

To figure out the plot, ask, What is the problem in the story? What events lead to its solution? What is the solution?

Title of story:

Who the characters are:

Where the story takes place:

What happens:

Event that presents a problem:

How the problem is solved:

THINK & WRITE

Each event in a plot is important. What would happen if one event were left out of the legend "Moon of Falling Leaves"?

THE REASON IT RAINED

By Janelle Adair
Read the story. Then use it to complete page 39.

The rains had poured down for days. Water dripped from the trees, the grass, and the bushes. Little animals hid in their holes, and a cold chill hung in the air.

In their houses, the villagers stayed close to their fires. "Will the rain ever stop?" they asked. At last a brave young woman named Marta spoke. "Give me a swift horse," she said, "and I will go in search of the reason it rains."

The villagers brought a strong white mare for Marta to ride. She galloped into the woods while the rain pounded against her. She had ridden for three days when she came to a clearing. There on a rock sat a tall young man dressed in green. His face was wet from crying. "Why do you cry?" Marta asked kindly.

"I have lost my way," he said, "and I am lonely and frightened. I fear I will never get out of these woods."

"Climb onto my horse," said Marta, "and I will take you to my village, where you will be safe and warm." But the young man couldn't move. Only when Marta promised to marry him was he able to leave the boulder. He climbed onto the horse, behind her.

As they rode, the weeping stopped. At that moment the rain stopped, too.

When they reached the village, they found that the people had prepared a feast of sweet cakes and berries to welcome Marta and the man. The bright sun once again warmed the earth, and the sky was blue.

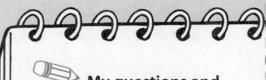

My questions and ideas as I read

Copyright © 1996 Scholastic Inc.

PLOT

Complete the plot map with information
from "The Reason It Rained."

To figure out the
plot, ask, What is the
problem in the story?
What events lead to
its solution? What is
the solution?

What was the problem?

How did the characters try to solve the problem?

What happened to help the characters solve the problem?

What happened that got in the way of solving the problem?

How was the problem solved?

What else could have gotten in the way of solving the problem in "The Reason
It Rained"? Describe the event, and tell how the characters dealt with it.

DESIGN A NATIONAL PARK FLAG

Flags use colorful pictures, symbols, and words to get information across. They're often used to identify special places—like national parks. Choose a park from the chart below and design a flag that tells something about it.

NATIONAL PARK HEADQUARTERS

If you don't see a park you like, find a list of national parks and choose your own. There are dozens more! So get out a piece of paper and draw your flag!

SIX GREAT NATIONAL PARKS

Name	State	Sights	Wildlife
Badlands	South Dakota	40-million-year-old fossils	bison
Biscayne	Florida	coral reefs	tropical fish
Crater Lake	Oregon	deep blue lake inside an inactive volcano	bald eagles
Kenai Fjords	Alaska	ice fields	mountain goats
Mammoth Cave	Kentucky	caves and underground rivers	bats
Olympic	Washington	a northern rain forest	elk

Copyright © 1996 Scholastic Inc.

Name

WILDLIFE DIAGRAM

The diagram below shows the parts of a fox.

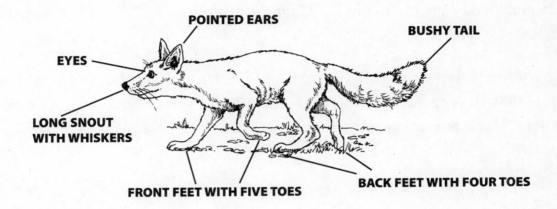

POINTED EARS

BUSHY TAIL

EYES

LONG SNOUT
WITH WHISKERS

FRONT FEET WITH FIVE TOES

BACK FEET WITH FOUR TOES

Add labels to each diagram below. Label as many parts of each animal as you can. If you can, give a short description of each part, based on your observations.

Name

ANIMAL CATEGORIES

Scientists put animals into categories. For example, all animals that have six legs are called insects. The animals on this page could also be grouped into other categories. For example, one category might be "Animals With Two Eyes." All four animals would fit into this category.

Make up four categories of your own for the animals in the pictures. List the animals that fit into each category. Each category may have from two to four members. Each animal may fit into more than one category.

Category:_____

_____

_____

_____

_____

Category:_____

_____

_____

_____

_____

Category:_____

_____

_____

_____

Category:_____

_____

_____

_____

IT'S IN THE TEXT

Read this page about birds from a science textbook.

BIRDS

Some soar; some swim. Some are as tiny as butterflies, and others have 8-foot wingspans. Birds are amazing. Probably the most amazing thing about birds is their ability to fly. As you learn more about birds, you will look at some of the characteristics that help them fly.

Characteristics of Birds

Beaks and Claws

There's no question about it—it takes a lot of energy to fly. Like other animals, birds get energy from food. Different types of beaks help birds get that food. Cardinals have strong beaks that they use to crack seeds open. Owls have beaks shaped like hooks that help them tear apart and eat small animals.

Owls also use round, sharp claws to catch food, but cardinals use their claws to perch on branches.

Feathers

All birds have feathers. The feathers birds use for flying are long and stiff. They are called contour feathers. Other feathers are short and fluffy. These feathers, called down feathers, keep birds warm. The down feathers are close to the bird's body. The contour feathers lie on top of the down feathers.

➡ How do you think contour feathers help a bird fly?

Eyes

Most birds have large eyes and can see very well. Their eyes help them find food and avoid flying into things.

On another sheet of paper, make a diagram of a bird that shows the characteristics you read about. Be sure to label your diagram. Include information about each characteristic in your labels. You should have at least four labels.

AN UNINVITED GUEST

Write the word from the box that best
replaces each underlined word or phrase.

burrow: a hole dug in the ground by an animal and used for shelter

territory: an area of land belonging to a particular animal

trail: series of marks that show the way to something

tracks: marks left by animals or people, such as footprints

range: an area of land on which an animal lives its entire life

predator: an animal that hunts other animals for food

prey: an animal that is hunted by another animal as food

raccoon: a small animal with masklike markings on its face

I spied animal <u>prints</u> (1) _____ leading to my closet. So I followed

the <u>path</u> (2) _____ to my closet door. I was surprised to find a

<u>small animal with a masklike face</u> (3) _____ looking up at me. It's

strange—animals usually spend their entire lives in their own <u>area</u>

(4) _____. Since it was hiding, maybe it thought I was an <u>animal</u>

<u>hunting for food</u> (5) _____. It shouldn't have felt like a <u>hunted</u>

<u>animal</u> (6) _____, since I mostly eat carrots. Maybe it was looking

for a <u>piece of land</u> (7) _____ to make its own. I'm glad it didn't dig

a <u>tunnel</u> (8) _____ through the mess on the floor.

You are taking a nature walk through the forest. Use at least four of the
words from the box to write about your experience.

ANIMAL FACTS

Use what you learned in "In Your Own Backyard" and *Secrets of a Wildlife Watcher* to complete the following informational posters.

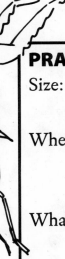

PRAYING MANTIS

Size:

Where you can find them:

What they eat:

Why they're useful to have around:

RACCOONS

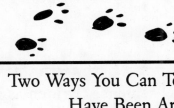

Where you can find them:

What they eat:

How they may be dangerous to humans:

OWLS & HAWKS

How you can find them:
Owls:

Hawks:

Two Ways You Can Tell If Animals Have Been Around

1. _____

   _____

2. _____

   _____

   _____

WRITER'S STYLE

Choose a spot in your neighborhood to visit and observe. Then write a guide to its wildlife, following the style of Jim Arnosky. Use the chart below to prepare your notes.

Place I observed:

Plants and animals I saw there:

Details I want to include:

My opening sentence (written as if speaking to a friend):

Did I address the reader as a friend?

Have I included accurate and descriptive details?

Will my descriptions help the reader imagine sights, sounds, or feelings?

Name

ANIMAL GROUPS

Look at the list of animals in the box. How could you group them? Be sure you put at least two animals in each group. Write what each group has in common at the top of the column.

When you categorize information, you notice what groups have in common.

owl	chickadee	trout	deer
coyote	skunk	rabbit	woodpecker
hawk	otter	fox	songbird

GROUP 1	GROUP 2	GROUP 3
coyote		

Look again at the list of animals. What other ways could you use to group them?

Name

AMERICA'S MOST WANTED INSECTS

by Mi Won Kim, from *Scholastic News*
Read the article. Then use it to complete page 49.

Who needs bugs? Believe it or not, you do! Many bugs are wanted—not dead, but alive. Here are some bugs that are helpful to people.

Pests Beware! Farmers and gardeners love praying mantises. These insects eat grasshoppers and other bugs that hurt plants. The fierce mantis holds its two front legs as if it is praying. But plant-eating bugs, watch out! A mantis has legs that are like jaws with sharp teeth. Gotcha!

A Winner of a Spinner When the silkworm is ready to turn into a moth, it spins a thread around itself and forms a cocoon. The thread is used to make a cloth called silk. Silk factories unwind silkworm cocoons and turn them into thicker thread. It takes about 20,000 cocoons to make one pound of silk cloth!

Watch Out for This "Lady"! Years ago, harmful insects nearly destroyed California's orange and lemon crops. Along came ladybugs to the rescue. They gobbled up the insects and saved the fruit trees. Today, ladybugs still munch on pests that hurt crops.

Just Call Me "Honey"! What's the big buzz about these bees? Honey! Honeybees make honey by gathering sweet liquid, called nectar, from flowers. They also help plants grow. As honeybees travel from one flower to another, they spread pollen. Without this service, flowers couldn't make new seeds.

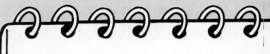

 My questions and ideas as I read

CATEGORIZE INFORMATION

Think of ways to group together the bugs you read about in "America's Most Wanted Insects." Fill in the boxes in the left-hand column with categories that apply to at least two of the bugs. Fill in the boxes in the right-hand column with the bugs that belong in those categories. The first box is filled in for you.

When you categorize information, you notice what certain things have in common.

GROUP	INSECTS IN THIS GROUP
Insects That Help Farmers	

THINK & WRITE

Make a list of six kinds of insects that you have seen or read about. Write down their characteristics—the way they move, where they live, and so on. Then categorize the insects.

PRE-PROJECT PLANNER

At the end of this unit, you will create a field guide. Turn to page 114 of your SourceBook, and read about that Project. From now until you begin the Project, think about what you'll need in order to do it. Also think about what you've learned in this unit that could help you.

1. Look back at one story in this unit that tells about an animal. What facts does it provide about the animal?

_____

_____

_____

2. Which of those facts would you put in a field guide?

_____

_____

3. Where could you get more information about the animal?

_____

_____

4. How could a park ranger help you put together a field guide?

_____

_____

_____

5. In the Workshops for this unit, you kept a nature log and drew a wildlife diagram. How could what you learned in the Workshops help you do the Project?

_____

_____

_____

NATURE'S WAY

Complete the word web by writing each word from the box in the correct list. You can use a word more than once.

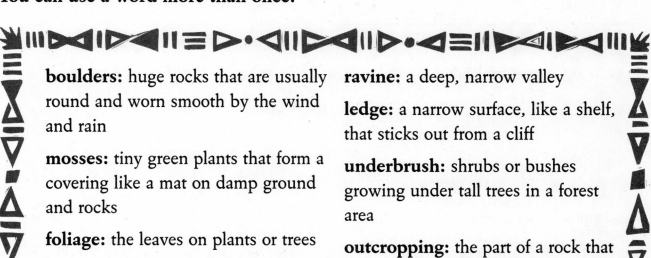

boulders: huge rocks that are usually round and worn smooth by the wind and rain

mosses: tiny green plants that form a covering like a mat on damp ground and rocks

foliage: the leaves on plants or trees

hollow: an area of land that is lower than the surrounding land

ravine: a deep, narrow valley

ledge: a narrow surface, like a shelf, that sticks out from a cliff

underbrush: shrubs or bushes growing under tall trees in a forest area

outcropping: the part of a rock that can be seen from the surface of the ground

WORDS ABOUT THE LAND

_____

_____

_____

A WOODED VALLEY

WORDS ABOUT PLANT LIFE

_____

_____

_____

WORDS ABOUT ROCKS

_____

_____

_____

In a magazine or catalog, find a picture—a drawing, painting, or photograph—of a forest scene. Use at least three of the words from the box to label the pictures.

SEND IT HOME

The narrator of *The Midnight Fox* is writing a letter to his mother telling her about his vacation. Help complete his letter.

Dear Mom,

I'm having a great time here! Each day I go to the woods to look for

(1) _____ . This is what she looks like: (2) _____

_____ .

What I really wanted to do was to find her den. I looked (3) _____ and

logs and stuck sticks in rotten logs. I found a (4) _____

_____, and a possum, but no den! Then one day I decided to go up the creek.

In the water I saw (5) _____ . Finally, I saw the black

fox, carrying a (6) _____ . Then, I spotted the baby

(7) _____ . He was tiny and woolly, and had a stubby nose. Suddenly

there was a noise. I did not want them to see me because the mother might think I had

discovered (8) _____ and would take her baby away. I decided I would

never go back to the den again. But I did see her (9) _____ .

I'll tell you more when I see you!

Love,

Tom

P.S. Don't get upset when you see my suitcase, because it's (10) _____

_____ .

HOW TO WRITE AN INFORMATIONAL STORY

Observe the habits of an animal or a person, and write a story using your observations. Use the chart to help you.

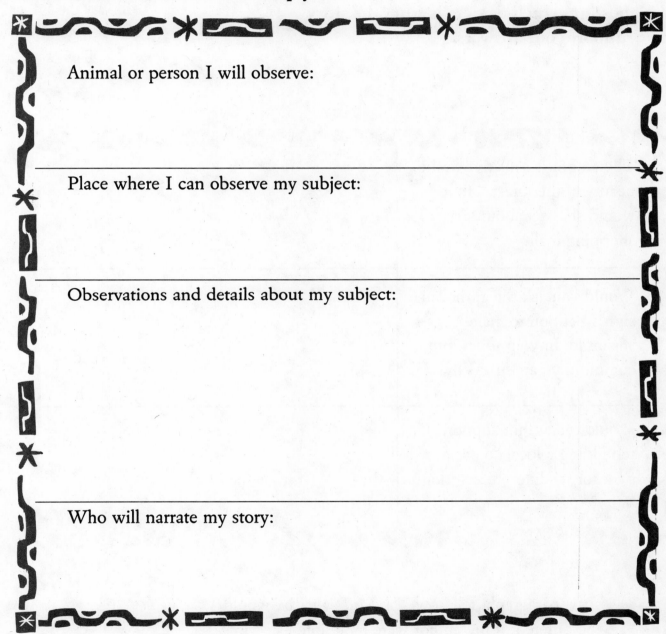

Animal or person I will observe:

Place where I can observe my subject:

Observations and details about my subject:

Who will narrate my story:

Will my story contain observations and details about an animal or person? Can I present the information clearly in a story?

Name

BE SLY, LIKE A FOX

Read the questions about *The Midnight Fox* on the left side of the chart. Then, on the right, answer the questions. Include details from the story that support your answers.

The author's viewpoint is the way the author feels about the subject.

The author is sensitive to the beauty of the forest. How would she feel about a shopping mall?	
Would you ask the author to sign a petition to make a vacant lot in your town into a community garden? Why?	
Would the author support rebuilding a local zoo as a park for wildlife preservation? Why?	

In a paragraph, tell how *The Midnight Fox* would be different if the author were more interested in Tom and less interested in the fox.

NATURE'S TELEVISION

By Sara Singh

As you read the story, write your questions and ideas about it in the column on the right. Then complete page 56.

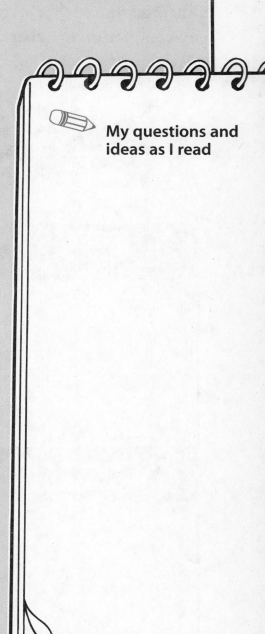

My questions and ideas as I read

"The television's broken again," said Celeste as she stomped to her room. "There's nothing to look at, nothing to do." She plopped herself down in front of the dining room window. It was May, and the rain had just stopped. There were two ugly gray birds hopping around outside the window. Celeste looked at them. "How boring. Just a couple of stupid birds. If the TV were working, at least I could watch something interesting," she said to no one in particular.

One of the birds flew to a nearby bush with a twig in its beak. It disappeared into the bush and then, after a few seconds, came out without the twig. The second bird landed on the bush, carrying an even bigger twig. It couldn't get the twig into the bush. It sort of backed up and went in backwards. Just its head and beak were sticking out—and the twig. The bird was pulling the twig into the bush. It was a struggle.

Celeste realized she was watching a show. It was like one of those nature programs on educational television—but better. She could see the birds bouncing, their heads bobbing. They were building a nest, a home. Now they were carrying a different material—dried grass.

"Nature puts on a pretty good show!" Celeste thought. "I never dreamed that watching birds build a nest could be so interesting. I guess there's more to life than watching TV."

EVALUATE AUTHOR'S VIEWPOINT

Examine the author's viewpoint in "Nature's Television" by completing the chart.

When you read, look for clues that tell what the author thinks about the subject.

AUTHOR'S VIEWPOINT ON TELEVISION	THINGS IN THE STORY THAT LET ME KNOW THIS

AUTHOR'S VIEWPOINT ON NATURE	THINGS IN THE STORY THAT LET ME KNOW THIS

 Write a continuation of "Nature's Television." Using the same author's viewpoint, tell what Celeste will do after the television has been repaired.

ORGANIZE YOUR INFORMATION

When you are recording a lot of information, organizing it in a table may be helpful.

Use the table below to record what you see in your environment. Use sketches or words.

PLANTS		
Trees	Bushes	Other Plants

ANIMALS		
Insects	Birds	Other Animals

DESIGN YOUR FIELD GUIDE

When you made your observations for your field guide, you probably took a lot of notes. To make your field guide, you will have to decide which information to include and how to arrange it.

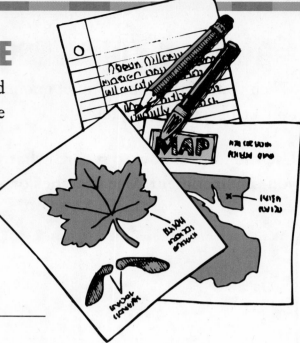

1. Which living things did you decide to include in your field guide? List at least eight things.

_____

_____

_____

2. In what order do you want these living things to appear in the field guide? Do you want to group them in any special way?

_____

_____

3. What kinds of details about each living thing do you want to include?

_____

_____

4. What facts from encyclopedias and field guides would you like to add?

_____

_____

5. Which drawings, diagrams, and maps would be useful to a person using your field guide?

_____

_____

WHAT DID I LEARN?

1. What are some of the responsibilities of a park ranger?

_____

_____

_____

2. What kind of skills or knowledge do you think a park ranger would need?

_____

_____

_____

3. What kinds of things did you do in the National Park Headquarters?

_____

_____

_____

4. What kinds of problems might you face as a park ranger? How would you go about solving them?

_____

_____

_____

5. On a separate sheet of paper, draw a picture of something you made or write about something you did in the National Park Headquarters.

BE A BETTER LISTENER

Use the following questions to help you be a better listener.

☐ Did I sit or stand up straight?

☐ Did I look at the person who was speaking?

☐ Did I pay attention to the person who was speaking?

☐ Did I use my imagination to picture what was being said?

☐ Did I think about the speaker's purpose?

☐ Did I ask questions if I didn't understand what was being said? Did I jot down notes of interesting and important points so that I could ask questions about them later? Did I use a "mind map" to capture ideas quickly?

☐ Did I ask the speaker to repeat important information to make sure I understood it correctly?

WHY DO I NEED TO LISTEN?	HOW CAN I LISTEN BETTER?	HOW WILL IT HELP ME?

Copyright © 1996 Scholastic Inc.

READER'S LOG

Keep track of books you read about managing information. When you've finished the unit, look over your list. Which book did you like best? Why was it your favorite?

Book Title	Author	Genre	Connection to Managing Information

My favorite book: _____

Reasons why I like this book best: _____

_____

_____

_____

LONG VOWEL SOUNDS

All the missing words in the puzzle below are like *local*
and *maple*. They have two syllables. The first syllable is accented.
The long vowel sound in the first syllable is spelled with a single letter that says its name.

**Use the clues to figure out the words. The highlighted letter in ( ) after each clue
tells you which long vowel you will hear in the first syllable. The circled letters
will spell two other words that follow the same pattern.**

1. a person; a _____ being (**u**)   __ __ __ ○ __

2. a large body of water, like the Atlantic (**o**)   __ ○ __ __ __ __

3. a couch (**o**)   __ ○ __ __

4. an eight-legged animal that spins webs (**i**)   __ __ __ __ __ ○

5. numbers like 2, 4, 6, 8, 10 (**e**)   __ __ __ ○ __

6. next year; opposite of past (**u**)   __ ○ __ __ __ __

7. risk; opposite of safety (**a**)   __ __ ○ __ __ __

8. the sound from a piano or guitar (**u**)   __ __ __ ○ __

9. a person who flies a plane (**i**)   __ __ __ __ ○

What words do the circled letters spell? _____ and _____

Surprise a friend or relative with a four-line rhyming
poem using the long *i* sound or the long *o* sound.

VOWEL SOUNDS + /r/

Use the vowel sound and the clues to help you write a word with a *vowel and* /r/. The first letter of each word is given to you. A given *vowel + /r/* can be spelled differently in different words.

1. /är/ as in *start*

large stringed instrument   h _ _ _

place to buy food   m _ _ _ _ _

place to live   a _ _ _ _ _ _ _ _

2. /ûr/ as in *skirt*

seeds grow in it   d _ _ _

clothing; a blouse   s _ _ _

carries its home around
on its back   t _ _ _ _ _

3. /âr/ as in *chair*

produces milk products   d _ _ _ _

fix it   r _ _ _ _ _

a flight of steps   s _ _ _ _ _ _ _ _

4. /âr/ as in *care*

to challenge   d _ _ _

mean look   g _ _ _ _

no shoes   b _ _ _ _ _ _ _

 Use the letters in the word *marketplace*. See how many words you can make that have /är/ as in *start*.

WHY DID THAT HAPPEN?

Write your answer about a cause or an effect on the line. For the last question, fill in the bubble beside the best answer.

1. Why did Ali Baba think his father was joking about taking a vacation in some parks?

   _____

   _____

2. Why did Ali Baba start to spend all his time looking for a bear?

   _____

   _____

3. Why did Ali Baba tell his parents he saw a bear the first time?

   _____

   _____

4. What happened when the first boy told Ali Baba he saw a bear?

   _____

   _____

5. Why was Ali Baba hearing lots of bear stories?
   - (a) because suddenly a lot of bears were turning up in the park
   - (b) because his small lie had grown into a big story
   - (c) because the other kids wanted to play a trick on him

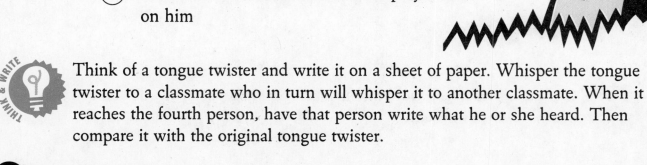

Copyright © 1996 Scholastic Inc.

 Think of a tongue twister and write it on a sheet of paper. Whisper the tongue twister to a classmate who in turn will whisper it to another classmate. When it reaches the fourth person, have that person write what he or she heard. Then compare it with the original tongue twister.

ALL THE FACTS

Fill in the bubble beside the best answer to each question, or write your answer on the line.

1. How are subjects arranged in an encyclopedia?
   - (a) numerically
   - (b) by subject
   - (c) alphabetically

2. Explain what the words on the upper outside corner of each page of an encyclopedia are for.

   _____

   _____

3. What can usually be found at the end of an encyclopedia article?
   - (a) the author's name
   - (b) a list of other articles related to the subject
   - (c) a list of the photographers who took pictures for the article

4. How could you use an encyclopedia to help you find information on bumblebees for your Project Field Guide?

   _____

   _____

   _____

Look up *mammal* in an encyclopedia. What information did you find? What related subjects are listed? Write a paragraph about how you would research this topic.

DOUBLE CONSONANTS

**All the answers below have double consonants.
The letter that comes before each double consonant is
a short vowel.**

A. Fill in the missing letters to learn about Bobby's favorite hobby.

1. His favorite sport is ___ ___ ___ m m ___ ___ ___.

2. His bathing suit is made of ___ ___ t t ___ ___.

3. He wears ___ ___ g g ___ ___ ___ underwater,
so he can see clearly.

4. He likes to splash around with ___ ___ ___ p p ___ ___ ___
on his feet.

B. Read the clues. Then fill in the missing letters.

1. a solid yellow spread to put on bread   ___ ___ t t ___ ___

2. a written note that can be mailed   ___ ___ t t ___ ___

3. a cake mixture of flour, milk, and eggs   ___ ___ t t ___ ___

4. warmer   ___ ___ t t ___ ___

5. having a sharp, unpleasant taste   ___ ___ t t ___ ___

EXTENSION

Use words with double consonants to write tongue twisters. For example, how
about a tongue twister about Betty's bitter batter?

SUFFIXES: *-ing* AND *-ed*

Complete each sentence below by adding the suffix *-ing* or *-ed* to the word on the left.

Remember that many one-syllable verbs ending with a consonant will double the consonant when *-ed* or *-ing* is added. Many one-syllable verbs that end with an *-e* will drop the *e* when *-ed* or *-ing* is added.

1. skid   The car _____ on the icy road.

2. crane   She was _____ her neck to see the parade
                 over the crowd.

3. scan   He _____ the book to see if it had information
                 about dinosaurs.

4. practice   She spent all her free time _____ free throws before
                 the basketball tryouts.

5. amaze   The special effects in the movie were _____ .

6. star   I _____ in the school play
                 last year.

7. plod   _____ through the deep
                 snow was hard and slow going.

 Make a list of five one-syllable words that can have the endings *-ing* and *-ed*
added. Challenge a partner to add the correct ending to each word.

COMPOUND WORDS

Write the small words that make up each compound word below. Next, write the meaning for each part of the compound word. Then write the meaning of the compound word.

1. someday

   first part: _____

   second part:_____

   meaning of first part: _____

   meaning of second part: _____

   meaning of compound word: _____

2. woodlands

   first part: _____

   second part:_____

   meaning of first part: _____

   meaning of second part: _____

   meaning of compound word: _____

3. outside

   first part: _____

   second part:_____

   meaning of first part: _____

   meaning of second part: _____

   meaning of compound word: _____

Write a paragraph using the above compound words and three new ones.

Name

LOOK IT UP

Fill in the bubble beside the best answer to each question, or write your answer on the line.

1. How might information be arranged in a textbook?
   - (a) by chapters
   - (b) by units
   - (c) alphabetically
   - (d) a and b

2. What appears in the front of a textbook that can help you find information inside the book?
   - (a) the author's name
   - (b) a table of contents
   - (c) an index

3. What appears at the end of a textbook that can help you find specific information in the book?
   - (a) the bibliography
   - (b) the table of contents
   - (c) the index

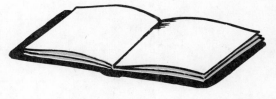

4. What are two clues within a chapter that might quickly tell you how information is arranged?

_____

Use a textbook to help you draw and label a diagram of a flower or a twig and its parts.

SPANISH AND NATIVE AMERICAN WORDS

Many words in English have been borrowed from Spanish or from Native American languages. Use the code to figure out which language each word in the box comes from.

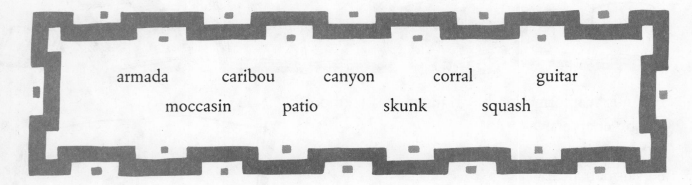

armada	caribou	canyon	corral	guitar
moccasin	patio	skunk	squash	

A = 2	F = 12	K = 22	P = 5	U = 15
B = 4	G = 14	L = 24	Q = 7	V = 17
C = 6	H = 16	M = 26	R = 9	W = 19
D = 8	I = 18	N = 1	S = 11	X = 21
E = 10	J = 20	O = 3	T = 13	Y = 23
				Z = 25

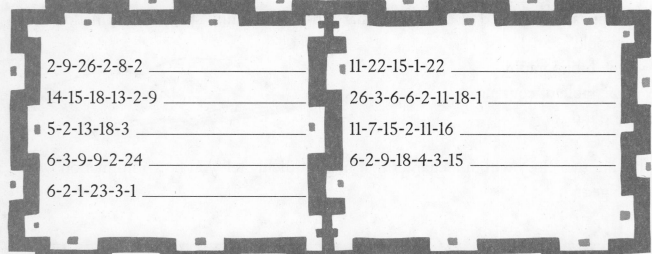

SPANISH

2-9-26-2-8-2 _____

14-15-18-13-2-9 _____

5-2-13-18-3 _____

6-3-9-9-2-24 _____

6-2-1-23-3-1 _____

NATIVE AMERICAN

11-22-15-1-22 _____

26-3-6-6-2-11-18-1 _____

11-7-15-2-11-16 _____

6-2-9-18-4-3-15 _____

Choose three words from each list. Write a context sentence for it.

Name

FIND THE CLUES

Use context clues to figure out the meaning of the underlined words.

1. Then the head <u>swivels</u> about, much as your head does.

   Context clues: _____

   Meaning of underlined word: _____

2. But a few of the pests may have a natural resistance to the poison spray. When these individuals breed, they will pass their <u>immunity</u> on to their young.

   Context clues: _____

   Meaning of underlined word: _____

3. "But that's impossible," you might say as you pick up the trash <u>strewn</u> all over the yard.

   Context clues: _____

   Meaning of underlined word: _____

4. Despite efforts to <u>deter</u> them, raccoons are increasing in number.

   Context clues: _____

   Meaning of underlined word: _____

Find another unfamiliar word in "In Your Own Backyard" and figure out its meaning using context clues. Then write a new sentence for the word, using context clues, and see if a partner can figure out the meaning of the word.

Name

WHY WRITE THIS?

Fill in the bubble beside the best answer to each question, or write your answer on the lines.

1. What was the author's purpose for writing "In Your Own Backyard"?

   (a) to entertain
   (b) to inform
   (c) to persuade

2. Why did you choose that answer?

   _____

   _____

3. Find one sentence from the article to support your answer.

   _____

   _____

4. Suppose the following sentences were in the article: "A praying mantis is the absolute best form of pest control. There is no substitute!" What could you say the author's purpose was from reading those two sentences?

   (a) to entertain
   (b) in inform
   (c) to persuade

THINK & WRITE

Create a poster that warns people of the dangers of raccoons. The purpose of your poster should be to inform and to persuade.

THE PLOT THICKENS

Fill in the bubble beside the best answer to each question.

1. Which is not a plot element?
   (a) the story problem
   (b) where the story takes place
   (c) events that lead to solving the problem
   (d) how the story is resolved

2. What was the problem in the story *The Midnight Fox?*
   (a) Tom was bored at his aunt and uncle's house.
   (b) Tom was scared of the fox.
   (c) Tom wanted to find the fox's den.
   (d) Tom didn't have any friends his age to play with.

3. What was one event that led to the solution to the problem?
   (a) The fox carried something in her mouth that looked like a frog.
   (b) The fox looked at Tom and froze for a moment.
   (c) Tom waited for the fox at the creek.
   (d) The fox watched her baby with satisfaction.

4. What was the solution to the problem?
   (a) Tom decided that nothing exciting would happen on his vacation, so he went home.
   (b) The fox was afraid of Tom and ran away.
   (c) Tom found a friend to come along with him and find the fox.
   (d) Tom found the den and was able to watch the fox and her baby.

Write a short letter to Tom suggesting a different solution to his problem.

GET THE DISCUSSION GOING

Use this organizer to get your discussion started.

1. The part I liked best was _____
   _____.

2. In the beginning I thought _____
   _____.

3. My favorite character was _____

   because _____.

4. The confusing part was _____
   _____.

5. I like the way the author _____
   _____.

6. I would change _____
   _____.

7. I didn't like _____

   because _____.

8. The book reminds me of _____
   _____.

PRESENT YOUR BOOK

Use this outline to present your book to the class.

Book Title _____ **Author** _____

Tell the main problem in your story. _____

_____

_____

Tell what the characters did to try to solve the problem.

_____

_____

Tell how the problem was solved. _____

_____

_____

Think of a different way you might have solved the problem.

_____

_____

How would this solution to the problem have changed the story?

_____

_____

_____

LISTEN FOR MAIN IDEA/DETAILS

As you listen, write down the main idea and details that support it.

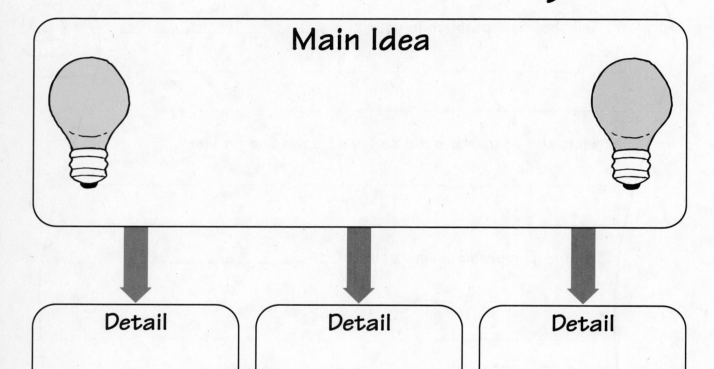

Main Idea

Detail

Detail

Detail

LITERACY-at-WORK
B O O K

IT TAKES A LEADER

COMMUNITY INVOLVEMENT

TABLE OF CONTENTS

It Takes a Leader

★ NEWSLETTER ★

Welcome to
It Takes a Leader

What do the President of the United States and the head of a town recycling committee have in common? They're both leaders who work to make changes in a community. In this SourceBook, you'll learn about all kinds of people who lead the way. Read on. You may be inspired to become a leader yourself!

Taking Charge

What issues are important to you? In this section, you'll meet some African-American heroes who took a stand on what was important to them. You'll also read a story by Natalie Babbit about an unlikely environmental hero.

Meet a young community activist!

Spread the Word

Get the message out! That's what the people in this section are doing. You'll read a story about a woman who spoke out to help coal miners in 1899. You'll also meet a nine-year-old boy who spoke out and made a difference in his city.

★ ★ NEWSLETTER ★ ★

Ideas in Action

Working together is an important part of reaching any goal. Here you'll read about how members of a

baseball team worked together to save the rain forest.

 Read letters written by kids who want the world to work together.

Meet Suki Cheong

Find out how this young newspaper editor covers the stories that she feels are important.

Things You'll Do

- What issues are important to your community? Take an *opinion poll* to find out.

- Learn the best way to get your message across when you create a *public announcement* about an issue that you care about.

- What's your opinion? Here's your chance to speak your mind and put together a *newspaper Op-Ed page.*

Let's Visit a Newspaper Office

Where's the best place to learn the thoughts and ideas of a community? Just visit a newspaper. You'll see the place where it's all put together.

Getting Started

We designed a medal to give to leaders who inspired us. We picked a word that describes a quality many leaders have. The trouble is, the medal maker left out some letters. Can you figure out what the missing letters are and complete the word?

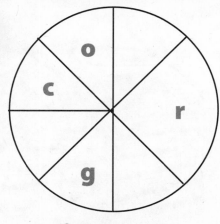

Answer: courage

WELCOME TO THE NEWSPAPER OFFICE

1. How do you think a newspaper is made?

_____

_____

_____

2. How do you think people decide what goes into a newspaper?

_____

_____

_____

3. What do you want to know about working in a newspaper office?

_____

_____

_____

4. How could you find out more about how a newspaper is run?

_____

_____

_____

STUDENT LOG

Here's a way to keep track of what you did in the Newspaper Office.

Fill in the chart when you visit the Newspaper Office.

Date	Time Spent	What I Did	What I Learned

SPEAK OUT!

Choose a word from the box to finish each sentence.

civil rights: the rights of personal liberty guaranteed to U.S. citizens by the Constitution and acts of Congress

boycott: a planned refusal to have anything to do with a person, group, or nation

activist: a person who takes action to help the community

oppressed: persecuted; governed unjustly

Underground Railroad: the name of the escape system for slaves in the South to travel north to freedom

abolitionist: a person who worked to abolish slavery

1. "Slavery has no place in a free land!" This person is an _____.

2. "If everyone stops buying its products, the company will have to change its ways." This person is talking about a _____.

3. "Citizens can vote." This person is stating one of his or her _____.

4. "First hide in here, then you will be conducted north to safety." This person is guiding someone through the _____.

5. "I believe in doing work to better my community." This person is an _____.

6. "I heard that some people were put down by their rulers for their beliefs." This person is speaking of people who were _____.

 You want to become an activist for stray animals in your community. Write a paragraph telling what you would do.

REMEMBER WHEN . . .

1. Why do you think the author wrote *Dinner at Aunt Connie's House*?

   _____

   _____

   _____

2. What part of this story is fantasy?

   _____

   _____

3. The women in the portraits had different ways of working for justice. Give two examples of these different ways.

   _____

   _____

   _____

   _____

4. Faith Ringgold is an African-American woman living today. How is she contributing to society?

   _____

   _____

   _____

WRITER'S STYLE

You will write a first-person biographical sketch about a famous person. Use the map below to jot down notes. When you write your sketch, select important and interesting details from your map.

EVENTS IN MY LIFE:

MY TALENTS:

MY NAME:

MY GOALS:

MY FAVORITE MEMORIES:

WRITER'S CHECK

Can I use the first-person voice throughout my sketch?
Do I know the most important events in the person's life?
Will it be clear to the reader why this person is important?

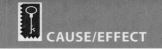
Name _____

CAUSES MAKE THINGS HAPPEN

In _Dinner at Aunt Connie's House_ we meet people whose actions had far-reaching effects. Under each woman's name, look at what she caused to happen. Write the effects that resulted. Complete the last box with information about a leader you choose—someone famous or someone you know.

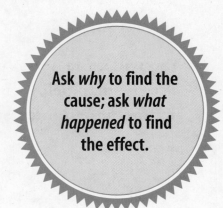

Ask _why_ to find the cause; ask _what happened_ to find the effect.

Mary McLeod Bethune	Harriet Tubman	
CAUSE	**CAUSE**	**CAUSE**
founded a college	joined the Underground Railroad	
EFFECT	**EFFECT**	**EFFECT**

THINK & WRITE

Choose another leader from the story. How did she make important changes come about?

BUCK'S NEW CAREER

By Reginald Curtis

As you read the story, write your questions and ideas in the column on the right. Then complete page 10.

 My questions and ideas as I read

Buck found an unmarked videocassette on the shelf. When he put it in the player, he found that it was a movie called *Lilies of the Field*. He was so absorbed in the movie, he didn't even hear his father walk in. Dad tapped his shoulder to get his attention.

"Hey, Dad," Buck said, putting the movie on pause. "This movie's really interesting. The lead actor is great."

"That's Sidney Poitier," Dad replied. "He was the principal African-American movie star of his time. He even won an Academy Award for this performance."

"Now I know what field I want to go into," Buck said. "I'll be an actor like Sidney What's-his-name."

"Poitier," Dad reminded him. "Well, nowadays Hollywood is more open to African-American actors. When Poitier first started, it wasn't that way at all. Nothing was open to him. He had a truly groundbreaking career. If you still want to be an actor in a couple of years, we'll talk about acting school."

Name

CAUSE/EFFECT

Read "Buck's New Career" on page 9. Then complete this chart by writing an effect for each cause. Ask yourself, What happened *because of* this event?

> The cause of an event is the reason the event happened. The effect is what happens as a result.

CAUSE	➡	EFFECT
Buck finds an unmarked video.		
Dad taps Buck on the shoulder.		
Buck admires Sidney Poitier.		
Sidney Poitier broke new ground as a leading African-American actor.		

Has watching TV ever caused you to change your mind about something? Write about the experience.

WORD CLUES

Read the following sentences from *Dinner at Aunt Connie's House*. Use context clues to figure out the meaning of each underlined word. Then write other possible meanings for the word.

Use text as well as picture clues to figure out the intended meaning of words that have more than one meaning.

1. Maria Stewart spoke next, about a woman's <u>right</u> to speak in public.

   <u>right</u> means _____

   other possible meanings:

   _____

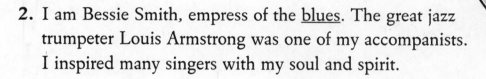

2. I am Bessie Smith, empress of the <u>blues</u>. The great jazz trumpeter Louis Armstrong was one of my accompanists. I inspired many singers with my soul and spirit.

   <u>blues</u> means _____

   other possible meanings: _____

3. I am Rosa Parks. I am called the mother of the civil rights <u>movement</u>. In 1955, I was arrested for refusing to sit in the back of the bus. That incident started the Montgomery bus boycott and inspired Martin Luther King, Jr., to devote his life to the civil rights movement.

   <u>movement</u> means _____

   other possible meanings: _____

 Write a sentence that uses one of the multiple-meaning words on this page in more than one way.

CONTEXT CLUES: MULTIPLE-MEANING WORDS

Read each sentence from "Buck's New Career" on page 9, and think about the underlined word. Write a definition for the word in the sentence. Then write another meaning for the same word and a new sentence that uses the other meaning.

Words often have more than one meaning. Look for context clues to figure out which meaning is being used.

SENTENCE	He was so <u>absorbed</u> in the movie, he didn't even hear his father walk in.	"Now I know what <u>field</u> I want to go into," Buck said.
WORD	absorbed	field
DEFINITION		
ANOTHER DEFINITION		
NEW SENTENCE		

Copyright © 1996 Scholastic Inc.

What other words do you know that have more than one meaning? Choose two words. Write two sentences for each word. In each sentence, use context clues to show which meaning you intend.

DESIGN A COMMUNITY SERVICE AD

Newspapers carry ads for products, but they also advertise community services and events. Think of a service that would help your community. It might be a clean-up effort, a food or clothing drive, or another idea you come up with. Design a newspaper ad that will make people want to pitch in to help.

NEWSPAPER OFFICE

HELPING OUT

Read the words in the box and their definitions. Then complete each sentence with a word from the box.

> **community:** all the people living together in one area
>
> **organization:** a group of people who work together for a particular purpose
>
> **overcome:** to struggle successfully against
>
> **process:** a series of actions that will achieve a purpose
>
> **accomplish:** to complete, achieve

1. Once he had _____ his fear of heights, Mike had a great time on the big roller coaster.

2. Everyone helps out at the recycling drive. It makes us feel like a

   _____.

3. Rivka's safety poster won first prize. Fitting in all the important information was hard to _____.

4. The scout troop had never held a Clean Up the Park Day, but the park ranger showed them the _____.

5. The whole school cleaned up the beach together. It took team spirit

   and _____.

 Use three words from the box to tell how your neighborhood could create a garden.

JUST DO IT!

1. What made Oog successful?

_____

_____

_____

2. The author tells how the shovel was invented. Do you agree or disagree with her explanation? Why?

_____

_____

3. How is this modern fable similar to an Aesop fable?

_____

_____

4. Rhiannon says that young people should help in community projects. Why does she think it is important for them to get involved?

_____

_____

5. If Rhiannon met the Giddywits, what advice might she have given them about throwing away garbage?

_____

_____

_____

FABLES

You will write a fable offering a solution to a modern problem. Your fable will need a moral, or lesson. It will also need at least two characters—one who sets a good example, and one who learns from his or her mistakes. The chart below will help you organize your ideas.

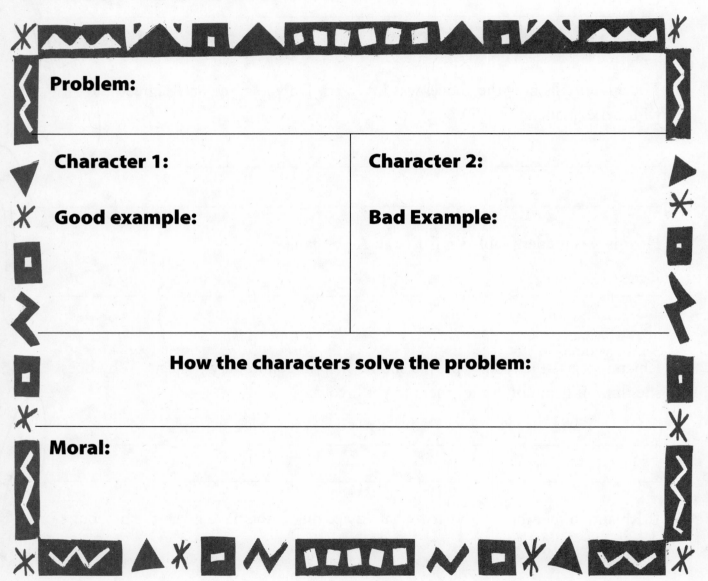

Problem:

Character 1:

Good example:

Character 2:

Bad Example:

How the characters solve the problem:

Moral:

Is the moral of my fable clear? Will my characters support the fable's message with a good and bad example?

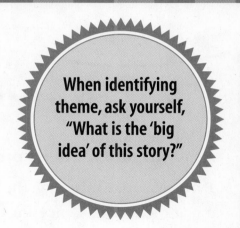
GET THE MESSAGE?

Underline the correct answers. Then answer the questions about "The Last Days of the Giddywit" on the lines.

When identifying theme, ask yourself, "What is the 'big idea' of this story?"

1. Which of these sayings best represents the theme of "The Last Days of the Giddywit?"

   a. A penny saved is a penny earned.

   b. Where there's a will, there's a way.

   c. A stitch in time saves nine.

   Why did you choose that answer?

   _____

   _____

2. Underline all of Oog's actions that helped you determine the theme.

   a. Oog hunted for eggs.

   b. Oog wanted to put the garbage outside.

   c. Oog wanted to live in the trees.

   d. Oog moved to a new cave.

   e. Oog invented a spoon.

   Why didn't you underline other answers?

   _____

   _____

3. In a sentence, state the theme of this story.

   _____

   _____

 The Giddywit babies grew up to be neat and tidy Oogites. What new problems do you think the Oogites will need to solve to take better care of their environment?

THE FINAL LOG JAM

by Brenda Malone
Read the story. Then complete page 19.

Every Monday morning, the beavers of Stump Lake met on a giant log. These meetings were called Log Jams. Each time they met, the beavers ended up dividing into two groups: the Nows and the Nos. The Nows liked new ideas. The Nos didn't like *any* ideas.

At one meeting, the topic was tree-cutting. Big Buck, one of the smartest Nows, presented his opinion. "We've taken down so many trees that we're going to have problems soon. I think we should start planting tree seeds. Then there will be trees for our youngsters to chew when they grow up."

All of the Nows agreed that this was a good idea. As usual, all the Nos wanted to wait. When the vote was taken, the Nows howled, "Now, now, now!" The Nos howled, "No, No, No!" Since the groups were equally divided, they couldn't reach a decision.

Big Buck decided that he'd had enough. "Come on, Nows," he said, "let's find a new home." So the Nows packed up and moved to a new lake, which they named Lake Renew. They planted a tree for every one they chewed down. The Nows have been there for many generations.

And what became of the Nos? Well, pretty soon they found themselves with no trees, no food, and no home. And no one has heard much from them since.

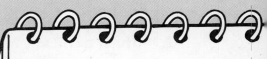

My questions and
ideas as I read

Copyright © 1996 Scholastic Inc.

THEME

Use this chart to help you find the theme of "The Final Log Jam." See how information about the characters helps you state the message of the story.

Writers sometimes use short stories to express a message to readers. You can look for that message, which is called a theme, by thinking about the characters and events in the story.

	What the Characters Say	What the Characters Do	What Happens to Them
THE NOWS			
THE NOS			
THEME			

MAKE A POLITICAL CARTOON

In a newspaper, the opinions of editors and readers are expressed in editorials and political cartoons. Pick an issue in the news that is important to you. Use an idea below, or come up with your own. Then create a political cartoon that shows your opinion on the issue.

NEWSPAPER OFFICE

ISSUES IN THE NEWS

speeding laws   animal rights
sports strikes   pollution
seat-belt laws   movie ratings
bike-helmet laws   school uniforms

POLL YOUR CLASSMATES

How can you find out your classmates' opinions on a subject? You can take a poll.
Ask everyone in the class the following question: What is your favorite subject in school? Two possible answers to this question are shown in the chart below. ("Other" means any subject other than the ones listed.)

Write three more possible subjects in the first column of the chart. Record each student's response by putting an X in the appropriate box under "Responses." Then add up the total number of X's for each response. Write those totals under "Total."

SUBJECT	RESPONSES	TOTAL
Science		
Other		

Which subject do most people in your class like best?

_____

_____

Copyright © 1996 Scholastic Inc.

GRAPH THE RESPONSES

On page 21, you polled your classmates and recorded the results. Now you have to present those results. One way to do that is with a graph.

Look at the graph below. The numbers along the left side represent numbers of students. Possible responses run along the bottom.

Fill in the other three subjects. Then above each subject, draw a bar that extends to the number of students who gave that response.

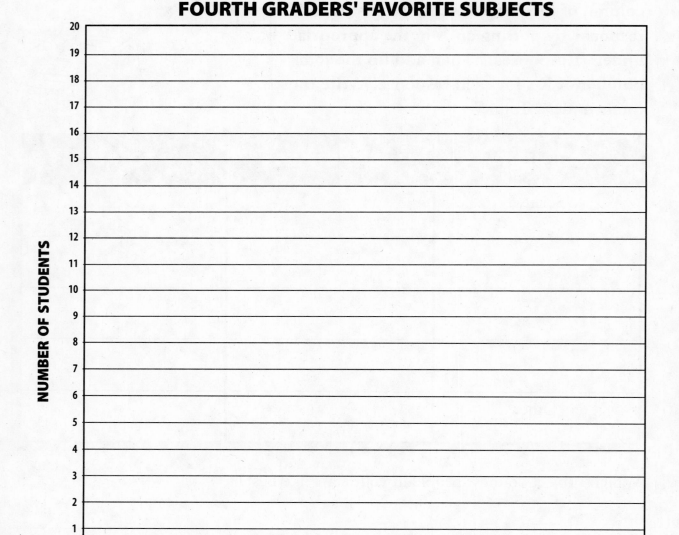

FOURTH GRADERS' FAVORITE SUBJECTS

NUMBER OF STUDENTS

20
19
18
17
16
15
14
13
12
11
10
9
8
7
6
5
4
3
2
1
0

Science   Other

FAVORITE SUBJECT

USE GRAPHS

The following graph shows the results of an opinion poll.

Study the bar graph. Then answer the questions below.

1. What was the purpose of this opinion poll?

_____

2. What do the numbers on the left side of the graph represent?

_____

3. What are the words at the bottom of each bar?

_____

4. Which breakfast food do the greatest number of people who were polled prefer?

_____

5. How many of the people polled prefer cereal? How many prefer muffins?

_____

CROSS THE LINES

Complete the puzzle using words from the box.

marching   strike   production   scab

raise   union   pledge

ACROSS

2. to stop work until certain demands have been met
4. the act of making something
6. a group of workers who join together to improve their working conditions and protect their interests
7. a solemn promise

DOWN

1. moving forward in a steady way, in step with others
3. a worker who takes the place of another worker on strike
5. an increase in salary

You're a TV reporter listening to speeches by people who want a safer place to work. Use at least three words from the box in your news report.

STRENGTH IN NUMBERS

Complete each statement.

1. People in the late 1800s needed coal because

_____

_____

_____

2. *Trouble at the Mines* is historical fiction because

_____

_____

_____

3. Mother Jones inspired the miners and their wives by persuading them to

_____

_____

4. Scabs could hurt the workers' cause, since they

_____

_____

_____

5. Rosie's mother was as brave as Mother Jones because

_____

_____

_____

HISTORICAL FICTION

You will write a short piece of historical fiction. Choose an exciting event from history, and imagine that you are there. Use this page to help you plan your piece.

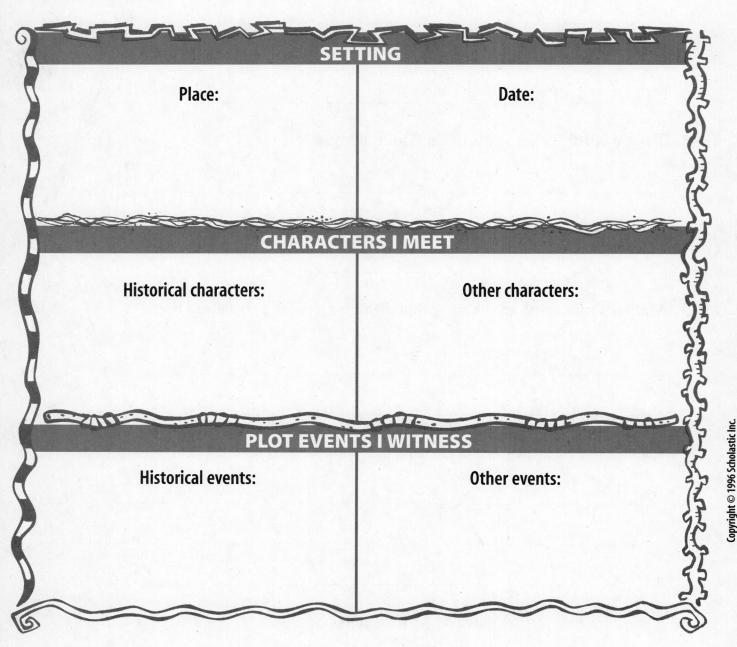

SETTING

Place:

Date:

CHARACTERS I MEET

Historical characters:

Other characters:

PLOT EVENTS I WITNESS

Historical events:

Other events:

Will my story be written from a first-person point of view?

Will I use real and fictional characters to tell about a historical event?

Are the historical details accurate?

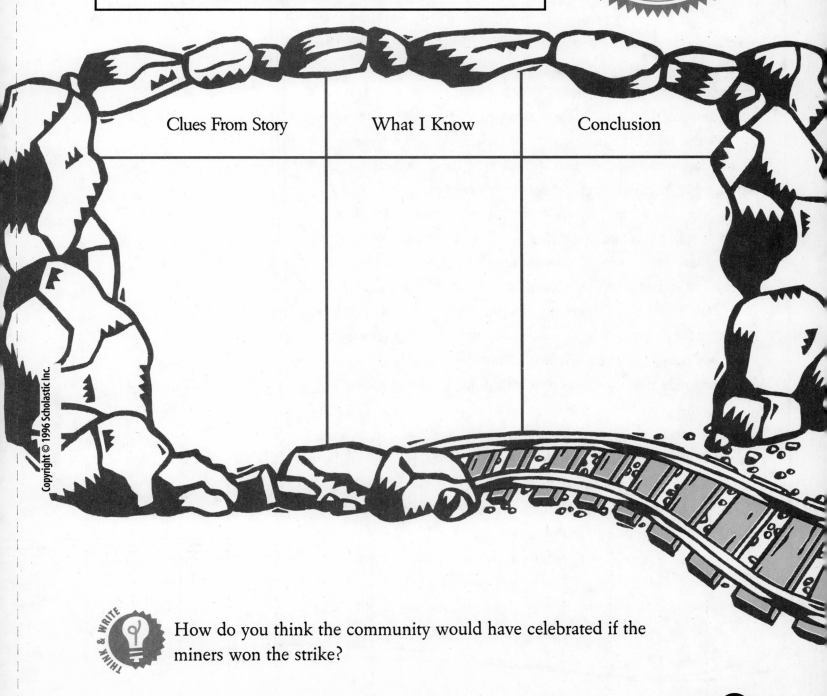
MINING CONCLUSIONS

Draw conclusions about one of the topics from *Trouble at the Mines* listed below.

> **Think about what you would do in a similar situation to draw conclusions about a story event.**

| what a miner does | women's part in achieving goals |
| life in a mining community | |

Clues From Story	What I Know	Conclusion

Copyright © 1996 Scholastic Inc.

THINK & WRITE

How do you think the community would have celebrated if the miners won the strike?

THE DAY OF THE DREAM

by Wallace Turner

Read the story and then complete page 29.

Bill knew it was going to be an important day. He had
never seen so many people. He held his father's hand as they
marched up the streets of Washington. It was August 28, 1963.

Bill knew it was important because it had been such a
struggle just to get there. His mother had heard that there
was going to be a rally for equal rights. "We have to be
there," she said. "It's time to stand up for what we believe in."

His father agreed, and so did a lot of their friends in
Atlanta. His parents decided to use money they had been
saving for a new sofa to buy bus tickets for the whole family.
Some families pitched their money together so they could
send at least one person to Washington.

Bill looked out at the enormous crowd. More than
200,000 people stood, listening to people talk about changing
the world. The mood was exciting, powerful, and angry.

Then came the moment everyone was waiting for.
Dr. Martin Luther King, Jr., came out. Bill could barely see
him, but he could hear every word. "I have a dream," Dr. King
pronounced, "that this nation will rise up and live out the true
meaning of its creed: We hold these truths to be self-evident,
that all men are created equal."

The crowd went wild. Bill saw his mother wipe away a
tear. His father looked strong and proud. He lifted Bill up and
said, "You hear, son? That's why we've come all this way.
Remember those words. They're the most important you'll
ever hear." Bill hugged his father and knew he was right.

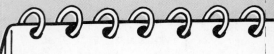

 **My questions and
ideas as I read**

Copyright © 1996 Scholastic Inc.

Name

DRAW CONCLUSIONS

Read "The Day of the Dream" on page 28. Think about the story clues listed in this chart. Add your own ideas to help you draw a conclusion based on each clue.

Readers can use story details to draw conclusions about characters and events. Use your own knowledge and experience to help draw and support your conclusions.

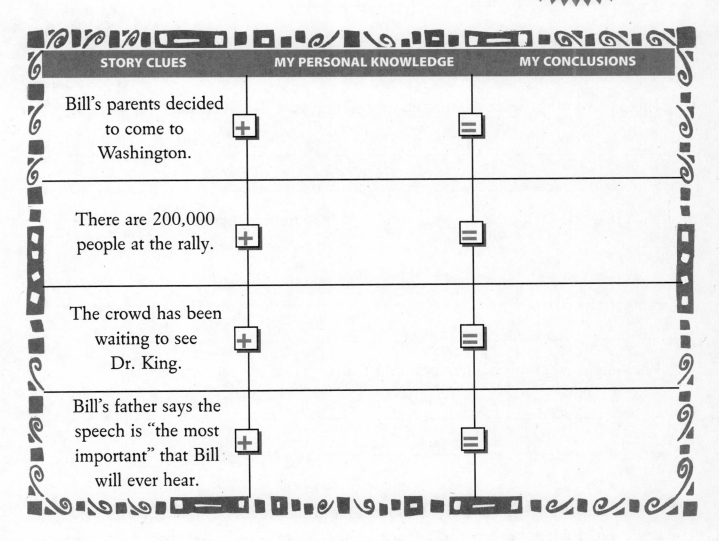

STORY CLUES	MY PERSONAL KNOWLEDGE	MY CONCLUSIONS
Bill's parents decided to come to Washington.	+	=
There are 200,000 people at the rally.	+	=
The crowd has been waiting to see Dr. King.	+	=
Bill's father says the speech is "the most important" that Bill will ever hear.	+	=

THINK & WRITE

Write a paragraph about a quotation in the story that means a lot to you.

WHAT A CHARACTER!

What if the characters from *Trouble at the Mines* were put in different situations? Think about what they are like and write how you think they would act.

Find a character trait by looking for a personal quality that comes up again and again.

1. What if Rosie had a chance to go to college?

   _____

   _____

2. What if the town's schoolteacher told Rosie's mother that the

   school was too small for the number of children who live in Arnot?

   _____

   _____

3. What if Uncle Jack gave the Wilson girls money to buy anything they wanted

   at the store?

   _____

   _____

4. What might other mining families do if Rosie's father got hurt on the job?

   _____

   _____

Choose a character from *Trouble at the Mines* that you wish you knew.
Write a letter to a friend about why you'd like to meet the character in person.

CHARACTER

Read "The Day of the Dream" on page 28. Use the diagram below to compare and contrast Bill and his father. Write words and ideas about each character in the appropriate space. In the overlapping area, write traits that both characters share.

You can learn about characters by thinking about what they say, what others say about them, and by what they do.

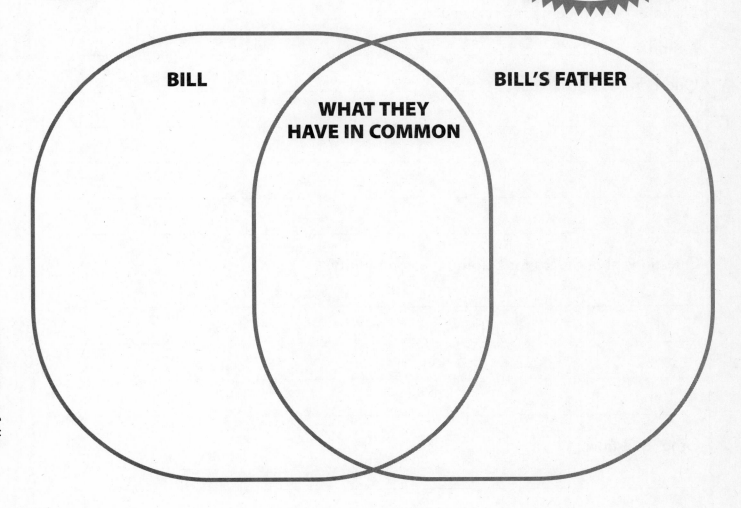

BILL

WHAT THEY HAVE IN COMMON

BILL'S FATHER

Write a story about a grown-up Bill. Think about his character in the story to help you decide what he might be like as an adult.

PLAN AN INTERVIEW

Reporters interview people to get the facts. Pick a leader in your community to interview: the mayor, the police chief, a school principal, or a teacher, for example. What would you ask that person in an interview for a newspaper article? List your ideas below.

NEWSPAPER OFFICE

Name of person being interviewed: _____

Job title: _____

Questions about the job: _____

_____

_____

_____

Questions about ideas for helping the community:

_____

_____

_____

Other questions:

_____

_____

_____

_____

TAKING IT TO CITY HALL

Study the definitions and complete the following story by filling in the correct word from the box.

council meeting: a gathering of elected officials who meet to make decisions about government

petition: a formal written request usually signed by those who support it

newspaper: a printed paper published daily or weekly that contains news

plan: a method or way of doing something that has been thought out beforehand

proposal: a plan that is presented to others for their consideration

Andy wanted to clean up the dirty park in his neighborhood and turn it into a great place to play. The first step in Andy's clean-up (1) _____ was to write a

(2) _____ stating what he thought should be done. Next, Andy asked people to support his idea by signing his (3)_____ . He told his story to a local

(4)_____ so people could learn about the park. At last, Andy was allowed to

present his idea at a (5)_____ in his town,

where a vote to clean up the park won!

Is there something in your community you'd like to change? Using three words from the box, write a notice to post in class about the change you'd make.

Name _____

YOU CAN MAKE A DIFFERENCE

1. What are two reasons for James Ale's success?

_____

_____

_____

2. The mayor told James that an old park had been vandalized. What might James have done if the new park had been vandalized?

_____

_____

3. Do you think that James would make a good lawyer or politician someday? Why?

_____

_____

_____

4. Why is a children's newspaper a good idea for both children and adults?

_____

_____

5. Do you think Suki Cheong might like to feature a story about James Ale? Why?

_____

_____

_____

What's the Big Idea?

Suki Cheong and everyone else at *Children's Express* brainstorm ideas for new stories. What if you sat in on one of these brainstorming meetings? What ideas do you have for different kinds of stories? List your thoughts below.

IDEAS FOR NEWS STORIES

Stories That Affect Young People

_____

_____

_____

Stories About My Community

_____

_____

_____

People to Interview

_____

_____

_____

Other Ideas

_____

_____

_____

INTERVIEW

You will interview a classmate about a school event, and write a summary of what you learned. Use this page to help you plan what to ask.

CLASSMATE TO INTERVIEW:

SCHOOL EVENT TO DISCUSS:

GENERAL QUESTIONS ABOUT MY CLASSMATE:

QUESTIONS ABOUT THE SCHOOL EVENT:

QUESTIONS ABOUT MY CLASSMATE'S OPINIONS:

Will the answers to my questions give information about the event and about my classmate's opinions? Can I present my classmate's opinions clearly in interview form?

WHICH HAPPENED FIRST?

Write a number from 1 to 6 in each box to show the order in which the following events from "James Ale" happened. Then add two other events from the story.

> Use signal words such as *first, then, next, suddenly, as, before,* and *after* to figure out the sequence of events.

☐ James Ale labels a map to show where the park could go.

☐ Bobby Adams is hit by a car.

☐ The children play in the street.

☐ James Ale telephones the mayor.

☐ James Ale meets the mayor behind a water tower.

☐ James Ale asks his father for advice.

An event that happens next:

_____

_____

An event that happens after that:

_____

_____

What do you think happened the first day James and his friend went to play in the park? Write a paragraph describing the day.

A FLAG FOR EVERYONE

by Brian Sung, from *Scholastic Action*

Read the article below. Use it to complete page 39.

Crystal Pike was worried. She saw garbage on the streets. She saw people fighting wars on TV. To Crystal, there seemed to be a lot going wrong in the world.

At first, Crystal didn't know how she could help. Then she had an idea. Why not make a symbol to unite the world?

After deciding what the symbol should be, Crystal created the first world flag. She put a green-and-blue background and a big picture of the earth on it. "That way, no one country stands out," says Crystal. "The message is clear. We all share the same world, and the world belongs to all of us."

Next, she showed the flag to her friends. They liked it. She showed the flag to more and more people. As time went on, stories about Crystal's world flag appeared in newspapers and on TV shows.

Crystal was invited to dedicate the flag to the Children's Peace Pavilion in Independence, Missouri. The dedication took place during the International Women's Conference for Peace. Crystal was the youngest speaker there.

Now Crystal wants to do more for the environment and for world peace. "I want to go to the U.N. and get people to listen to my message," says Crystal.

Crystal wants peace to happen. She realizes it is idealistic to hope that the flag can unite the world, but that doesn't mean she'll stop trying. She also knows that getting what she wants won't be easy.

"It's been hard so far," Crystal admits. "The last five years have been a lot of work. But I guess that's why our motto is 'Make a Difference.' Because you *can* make a difference."

My questions and ideas as I read

"A Flag for Everyone": by Brian Sung from SCHOLASTIC ACTION® October 8, 1993. Copyright © 1993 by Scholastic Inc. Reprinted by permission. Copyright © 1996 Scholastic Inc.

Name

SEQUENCE

In the boxes, write the most important events from "A Flag for Everyone" to show the correct order.

Sequence is the order in which events occur in a story. Look for words like *first, next, then,* and *last* to show sequence.

At first,

Then,

After that,

Next,

Later,

Finally,

What might Crystal Pike do next in her effort to unite the world? Write a plan that includes three steps Crystal might take.

CREATE A PHOTO SERIES

NEWSPAPER OFFICE

A newspaper will sometimes publish a series of photos and captions on a certain theme. Think of your own theme for a photo series. It can be the environment, sports, local heroes, or any other newsworthy topic that interests you. Cut photos from newspapers and magazines. Glue them to a large sheet of paper. Then write captions and create your page. Use this sheet to help you organize your ideas.

Title of photo series _____

Caption 1 _____

_____

Caption 2 _____

_____

Caption 3 _____

_____

Caption 4 _____

_____

Caption 5 _____

_____

IDENTIFY PUBLIC SERVICE ANNOUNCEMENTS

When you listen to the radio or watch TV, you hear many different kinds of messages. You might hear news reports, advertisements, or public service announcements. The purpose of public service announcements is to provide useful information to the community.

Below is a list of announcements that you might hear on the radio. Circle the ones that are public service announcements.

1. A news report about a bill passed by the state Senate

2. An announcement telling when a neighborhood block party will take place

3. An advertisement for Bill's Buttermilk Pancake Mix

4. A long-range weather report for your state

5. A notice that schools will be closed in your city because of a major snowstorm

6. An announcement that doctors will be doing free blood-pressure checkups at the mall

7. An announcement that a department store is having a big sale tomorrow

8. A story about a baby bear that was born at the local zoo

WRITE A PUBLIC SERVICE ANNOUNCEMENT

Look back at the public service announcements you found on page 41. Choose one. Think about what the public would need to know about that topic.

Write a public service announcement about your topic. Tell who is sponsoring the announcement and the reason for the announcement. Give the people listening all the information they'll need. Use catchy words to get your audience's attention.

USE NONPRINT MEDIA

Read the following transcript from a television news report. Then answer the questions.

SIX O'CLOCK NEWS

Amy Ogisu: I'm here in Dallas talking to a young gymnast who could tell all of us a thing or two about hard work and dedication. Sidonie Reed has been practicing her flips, backbends, and splits every day for more than seven years. Why is she doing all this hard work? She's hoping to make the next U.S. Olympic team. Hi, Sidonie. You're doing some pretty impressive things on that beam.

Sidonie: Um, thanks. I hope the judges will be as impressed as you are.

Amy: You've already won several national competitions this year. How much time do you spend training?

Sidonie: On school days I usually practice two or three hours, and on weekends I sometimes practice six or seven hours a day.

Amy: How do you find time for your schoolwork?

Sidonie: It's not easy! But gymnastics definitely teaches you to discipline yourself, so I think I can concentrate better.

Amy: Do you think you'll be ready for the Olympics in two years?

Sidonie: I sure hope so. That's my main goal in life right now.

Amy: Well, good luck and thanks for taking the time to talk to us. You certainly have a gold-medal attitude!

1. Where does the news story take place?

   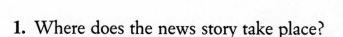
   _____

2. Who is the story about?

   _____

3. What does the news report tell about this person?

   _____

4. What are some differences between reading a transcript and actually watching a news report on TV?

   _____

   _____

MEANING THE SAME THING

Read each sentence. Choose a word from the box that has the same meaning as the underlined word or phrase in each sentence.

---

segregation: the separation of one group from the rest of society

apathetic: having little interest; indifferent

stand: a firm opinion about an issue

opposing: being against something; resisting

humiliations: offensive, insulting acts

hostility: resistance; conflict; ill will

---

1. The team suffered many <u>embarrassments</u> during its ten-game losing streak. _____

2. Leah and Sarah were so glad when they found out they were not on <u>conflicting</u> sides of the tug of war. _____

3. The whole team decided to take a <u>position</u> on why the new rule was unfair. _____

4. The <u>separation</u> of schools by race is against the law. _____

5. My sister is <u>unconcerned</u> about whether our room is messy or neat. _____

6. The <u>anger</u> displayed by the defeated coach was felt by all the players. _____

THINK & WRITE Pretend you fell asleep and woke up in a land where everybody was exactly the same. Using three words from the box, write about challenges you might face.

BATTER UP!

1. Why isn't there a Negro baseball league today?

_____

_____

_____

_____

2. Would you consider Branch Rickey a leader? Why?

_____

_____

_____

_____

3. Would you want Pee Wee Reese to be your friend? Why?

_____

_____

_____

4. If Pee Wee Reese hadn't supported Jackie Robinson, do you think Jackie would have given up his goal of staying on the team?

_____

_____

_____

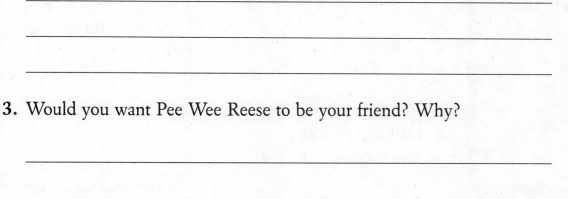

NONFICTION

Teammates gives you information about a real event by telling it in the form of a story. You will write a nonfiction story based on an article from a newspaper. This drawing will help you plan your story. Run from first base to home plate. Write your answers inside each base.

SECOND BASE
What happens first?

THIRD BASE
What happens next?

FIRST BASE
What is the article about? Who are the characters?

HOME PLATE
How does the story end?

WRITER'S CHECK
Can I present real people and events in story form?
Is it clear when and where the story takes place?

WHAT'S THE PURPOSE?

On the chart, write what you think the author's purpose was for writing *Teammates*. Using events that took place in *Teammates*, write the reasons for your choice.

To understand the purpose, ask yourself, Why did the author think it was important to write about this information?

AUTHOR'S PURPOSE:

REASONS WHY:

 How might the story change if the author's purpose were to describe how Jackie and Pee Wee became friends?

No Limits

by Wayne Coffey, from *Scholastic Action*

Read the biography below. Use it to complete page 49.

What are the odds of making the big leagues with one hand? Most people thought Jim Abbott should forget about even trying. These people had no idea that Jim has as much courage in him as he has talent in his left arm.

Even as a youngster in Flint, Michigan, Jim didn't listen to what people were saying. He focused on what he could do, not on what he couldn't. In first grade he threw away the artificial hand he'd been wearing. Soon, he could tie his shoes and even play baseball without it.

Mike and Kathy Abbott helped their son learn to deal with his disability. They encouraged him to make friends and play sports. They told him if he worked hard in school and did his best, that was all anyone could ask.

In baseball, many players thought Jim wouldn't be able to throw them out. They were wrong. Besides having a 90-mile-per-hour fastball and a sharp breaking ball, Jim made himself into a terrific fielder.

After high school, Jim pressed on to become a star pitcher at the University of Michigan. In 1988, his pitching helped the United States win an Olympic gold medal. Eventually Jim became one of the premier pitchers in the American League—without spending one day in the minor leagues!

Jim knows he has a valuable message to share, particularly for people with a disability. He tells them that if you believe in yourself, if you give everything you've got—in school, in sports, in everything—then you won't have any disability at all.

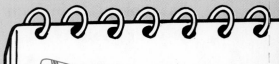

My questions and ideas as I read

"No Limits" by Wayne Coffey from SCHOLASTIC ACTION® October 22, 1993. Copyright © 1993 Scholastic Inc. Reprinted by permission. Copyright © 1996 Scholastic Inc.

EVALUATE AUTHOR'S PURPOSE

Read this checklist about "No Limits." Write a ✔ to answer yes or no to each question. Then answer the questions below.

Does the author...

As you read, ask yourself, "Why did the author think it was important to include this information?"

Yes   No

☐   ☐   try to convince people that they should learn the game of baseball?

☐   ☐   try to convince people to watch baseball on TV?

☐   ☐   tell about Jim Abbott's life and his determination to do well in sports?

☐   ☐   encourage people to believe in themselves?

☐   ☐   explain what it means to be a parent?

☐   ☐   explain how to throw a 90-mile-per-hour fastball?

1. What was the author's main purpose in writing?

_____

_____

2. What information in the biography helped you decide the author's main purpose?

_____

_____

Think of a sport that you enjoy and write a paragraph that either informs, persuades, or entertains your readers.

Name

PRE-PROJECT PLANNER

At the end of this unit, you and your classmates will be writing letters to the editor and putting them together to create an Op-Ed page for a class newspaper. Read about the Project on pages 114–119 of your SourceBook. Think about what you'll need to do before creating your Op-Ed page. Start looking at the Op-Ed page of your local newspaper. Notice what topics people write about.

Answer the following questions to help you prepare for the Project.

1. Think back to "Eye on the Prize" and "James Ale." What community issues were important to the young people in these selections?

   _____

   _____

2. What important community issues did Suki Cheong mention in her interview?

   _____

   _____

3. In the Workshops, you conducted a public opinion poll and wrote a public service announcement about important community issues. How could what you did in the Workshops help you write a letter to the editor?

   _____

   _____

4. James Ale did a great deal of research and preparation before presenting his message to the mayor and town administrator. Make a list of things you will have to do to prepare for writing your letter.

   _____

   _____

RAIN FOREST RIGHTS

Complete the letter with the correct words from the box.

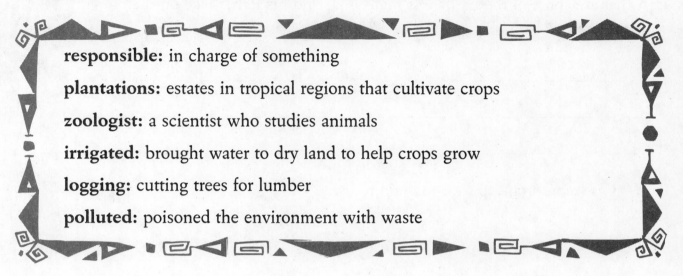

responsible: in charge of something

plantations: estates in tropical regions that cultivate crops

zoologist: a scientist who studies animals

irrigated: brought water to dry land to help crops grow

logging: cutting trees for lumber

polluted: poisoned the environment with waste

Dear Tamika,

Has your class learned about what's happening to the rain forests? People are clearing the land by (1) _____ it. They then build (2) _____ on land that must be (3) _____ , so that the crops can thrive. Any (4) _____ knows that the animals living in the rain forest will lose their homes. Our teacher said that plants and animals cannot survive once the air and water become (5) _____ . She said (6) _____ people must work to change this. I want to help. I hope you do, too.

Your friend,
Angela

You are a TV reporter. Write a report about rain forests for the evening news. Use at least three words from the box.

FIGHTING THE GOOD FIGHT

1. What are some of the hardships that Omar and his father face on their long walk?

_____

_____

_____

2. Why is it important to save the rain forest?

_____

_____

_____

3. Why do you think the governor tells Omar there is nothing to worry about?

_____

_____

_____

4. What are the similarities between Pu Lan and Wang Lin from *Dear World* and Omar?

_____

_____

Name

WRITE A LETTER REQUESTING CHANGE

You will write a letter requesting a change you would like to see in your community. Use the letters in the *Dear World* collection as models. The chart below will help you organize your information.

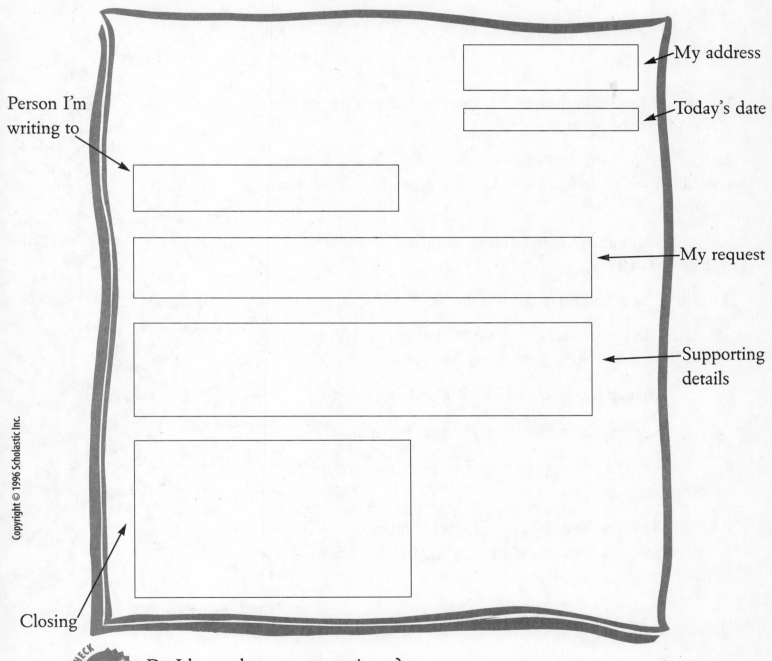

My address

Today's date

Person I'm writing to

My request

Supporting details

Closing

Do I know the person to write to?
Can I state my request clearly?
Will I include details that support my ideas?

Name

WHAT'S IMPORTANT?

Read the sentences below from *Save My Rainforest*. If a sentence contains important information about saving the rain forest, write an *I*. If it is unimportant, write a *U*.

> Important information tells you more about the main idea of the selection.

1. _____ They find a fruit stand where a woman with long braids sells them tall glasses of pineapple drink.

2. _____ "We need to tell him to save the rain forest so there will still be a rain forest in Mexico for us when the children grow up."

3. _____ "All kids have good ideas, but usually people don't listen to them."

4. _____ Omar had forgotten—today he is nine!

5. _____ An announcer comes on television to say there has been a terrible earthquake in Mexico City.

6. _____ They have traveled 870 miles and they are tired.

7. _____ Cutting down the forest changes the climate.

8. _____ Omar also learns that medicines come from the rain-forest plants.

9. _____ The President had promised that no more rain-forest creatures would be caught and sold, but he has broken his promise.

Why does Omar think it's important to keep fighting? List the important information that helped you answer the question.

THE KIDS OF KAP

by Loni Spanner

Read the story, then complete page 56.

A group of friends sat in a school cafeteria in Closter, New Jersey. While they were eating, one girl picked up a cup and said, "You know, this cup is made of polystyrene. That stuff is terrible for the environment."

"Yeah," agreed her best friend. "It doesn't decompose. That means it takes up space in landfills. And if you burn it, the fumes cause air pollution."

"Our school really shouldn't use any polystyrene at all," another friend added. "Let's take action."

The friends knew that there is strength in numbers. So they encouraged others to join their new group, called Kids Against Pollution (KAP). By their first meeting, 19 students had joined the group. Everyone had ideas for strategies.

"We should make posters to get the school's attention."

"Let's get school officials to start a ban on polystyrene."

They picked the best plans and went ahead. They pointed out the problems with polystyrene and identified alternatives. They were calm and professional. And in the end, they were successful. The school district agreed to the ban.

Since that time, KAP chapters have been organized throughout the United States and in other countries. The students fight to protect the environment. Their motto says it all: "Save the Earth, Not Just for Us, but for Future Generations."

My questions and ideas as I read

Name

IMPORTANT/UNIMPORTANT INFORMATION

Write a summary of the article "The Kids of KAP" that could be stored in a computer fact file. Your summary should contain only the important information in the article. On the notepad next to the computer, jot down some unimportant details that you will leave out of your summary.

> Not all information in an article is important. How can you tell which points in an article are important? If you need to use a piece of information to summarize an article, it's important.

Article: "The Kids of KAP"
Author: Loni Spanner
Summary:

Unimportant Details

Why do you think writers include some unimportant information? What would it be like to read an article that had only important information?

CHOOSE YOUR ISSUE AND STATE YOUR OPINION

In the box below, write the issue that you've chosen for the letter you will contribute to the class Op-Ed page. After you do your research on the issue, write your opinion about the issue. List three facts you learned that helped you form your opinion.

My opinion on the issue:

Facts that support my opinion:

LETTER TO THE EDITOR CHECKLIST

When you finish the first draft of your letter to the editor, use the chart below to see how you can improve it before contributing it to the class Op-Ed page.

ITEM	YES/NO	HOW TO IMPROVE
Did I include my address and the date?		
Is the letter addressed correctly?		
Did I follow the organization of my outline?		
Did I state my opinion clearly?		
Is my opinion supported by facts?		
Did I give suggestions for action?		
Did I use the correct closing?		

WHAT DID I LEARN?

1. What are the steps involved in putting out a newspaper?

_____

_____

_____

_____

2. What kinds of skills would it be important for a reporter or news editor to have? for a production person to have?

_____

_____

_____

_____

3. What kinds of problems might you face if you worked in a newspaper office?

_____

_____

_____

_____

4. On a separate sheet of paper, draw a picture or write about something you did in the Newspaper Office.

BE A BETTER TEAM MEMBER

Use the following questions to help you be a better team member.

- [ ] Do I listen to what others on my team have to say? Do I avoid interrupting when someone else is talking?

- [ ] Do I share my opinion honestly but kindly?

- [ ] Do I help others with the things I'm good at? Do I allow others to help me with the things *they* are good at?

- [ ] Do I do my fair share of any team task?

- [ ] Do I help think of ways to fairly divide team responsibilities?

- [ ] Do I encourage my teammates to do their best?

WHY DO I NEED TO BE PART OF A TEAM?	HOW CAN I BE A BETTER TEAM MEMBER?	WHAT ADVANTAGE WILL IT GIVE ME?

Copyright © 1996 Scholastic Inc.

READER'S LOG

Keep track of books you read about community involvement. When you've finished the unit, look over your list. Which book did you like best? Why was it your favorite?

Book Title	Author	Genre	Connection to Community Involvement

My favorite book: _____

Reasons why I like this book best: _____

_____

_____

_____

WORDS WITH /ou/, /ô/, /o͞o/, /o͝o/

The sound /ou/ can be spelled like *brow* or *couch*; /o͝o/ can be spelled like *during* or *looked*: /o͞o/ can be spelled like *rude* or *cool*; and /ô/ can be spelled like *brought* or *audience*. The definitions below all name words with one of these sounds.

Choose the correct word from the box for each definition below. Write the letters of the word on the lines. Then answer the riddle below.

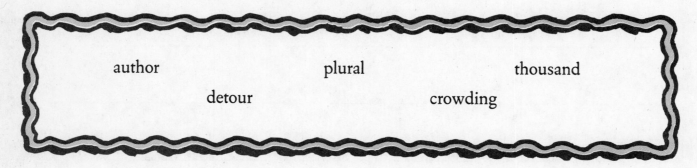

author   plural   thousand

detour   crowding

1. different route

$\underline{\hspace{0.3cm}}\ \underline{\hspace{0.3cm}}_3\ \underline{\hspace{0.3cm}}_4\ \underline{\hspace{0.3cm}}\ \underline{\hspace{0.3cm}}\ \underline{\hspace{0.3cm}}_5$

2. cramming into a small space

$\underline{\hspace{0.3cm}}\ \underline{\hspace{0.3cm}}\ \underline{\hspace{0.3cm}}\ \underline{\hspace{0.3cm}}\ \underline{\hspace{0.3cm}}\ \underline{\hspace{0.3cm}}\ \underline{\hspace{0.3cm}}_2\ \underline{\hspace{0.3cm}}_6$

3. ten times one hundred

$\underline{\hspace{0.3cm}}\ \underline{\hspace{0.3cm}}\ \underline{\hspace{0.3cm}}\ \underline{\hspace{0.3cm}}\ \underline{\hspace{0.3cm}}\ \underline{\hspace{0.3cm}}\ \underline{\hspace{0.3cm}}_{10}\ \underline{\hspace{0.3cm}}_{11}$

4. more than one

$\underline{\hspace{0.3cm}}\ \underline{\hspace{0.3cm}}\ \underline{\hspace{0.3cm}}_1\ \underline{\hspace{0.3cm}}\ \underline{\hspace{0.3cm}}$

5. a writer of books

$\underline{\hspace{0.3cm}}\ \underline{\hspace{0.3cm}}_9\ \underline{\hspace{0.3cm}}\ \underline{\hspace{0.3cm}}\ \underline{\hspace{0.3cm}}_8\ \underline{\hspace{0.3cm}}_7$

Now answer the riddle. Find the letter that goes with each number. Write the letter on the line.

This train had many conductors, but no cars or tracks.

It is the $\underline{\hspace{0.3cm}}_1\ \underline{\hspace{0.3cm}}_2\ \underline{\hspace{0.3cm}}_3\ \underline{\hspace{0.3cm}}_4\ \underline{\hspace{0.3cm}}_5\ \underline{\hspace{0.3cm}}_6\ \underline{\hspace{0.3cm}}_7\ \underline{\hspace{0.3cm}}_8\ \underline{\hspace{0.3cm}}_9\ \underline{\hspace{0.3cm}}_{10}\ \underline{\hspace{0.3cm}}_{11}$ Railroad.

EXTENSION Think of words with /ou/, /ô/, /o͞o/, and /o͝o/ that begin and end with the same sound, such as *mouse*, *Morse*, and *moose*. See how many examples you can come up with.

Name

FINAL SCHWA + *r, l,* AND *n*

Some words have an unstressed final syllable that contains the schwa sound—for example *clever* and *American*. Read the clues and fill in the answers. The first group names family members; the second group names jobs; the third group names people from around the world.

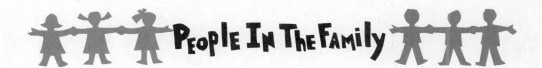

1. This person is a boy with a sister. _____

2. This person is the child of an aunt and uncle. _____

3. This person is a female parent. _____

4. This person argues cases in court. _____

5. This person helps us to get well when we are sick. _____

6. This person helps schoolchildren to learn. _____

7. a person from the country known for koala bears and kangaroos _____

8. a person from the continent directly south of North America _____

9. a person from the European country that is shaped like a boot _____

EXTENSION Think of other words with the final schwa+ *r, l,* or *n* that belong in the above groups. Then make up clues for these words. Challenge a friend to figure out the answers.

Name

WHAT DO YOU MEAN?

Read the paragraph below, paying special attention to each underlined word. Then fill in the bubble next to the best definition.

And the next morning, instead of climbing trees to look for eggs, he took Mrs. Oog by the (1) <u>hand</u> and went away, a long way off, miles and miles through the (2) <u>wild</u>, sweet land, and came after many days to a little cave just right for two. "This is the (3) <u>ticket</u>," he said to Mrs. Oog. "We'll live on nuts and berries and the very (4) <u>occasional</u> rabbit."

1. In the context of the sentence, the word *hand* means
    - (a) part of a clock
    - (b) part of the body
    - (c) penmanship

2. In the context of the sentence, the word *wild* means
    - (a) cruel
    - (b) uncontrolled
    - (c) natural

3. In the context of the sentence, the word *ticket* means
    - (a) the right spot to be
    - (b) entry to a musical show
    - (c) punishment for parking illegally

4. In the context of the sentence, the word *occasional* means
    - (a) special
    - (b) taking place at certain times
    - (c) only once in a while

Write two sentences each using the word *corners*. Use context to show two different meanings of the word.

Copyright © 1996 Scholastic Inc.

LET'S RAISE SOME MONEY

The graph below presents the results of a student vote. Study the graph and answer the questions below.

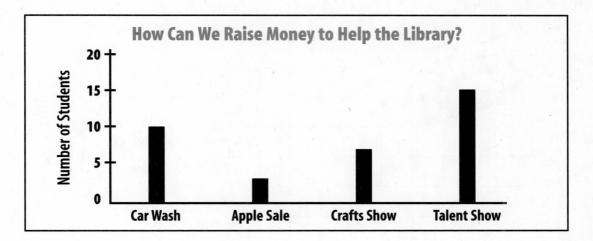

How Can We Raise Money to Help the Library?

1. What is the purpose of this graph? _____

   _____

2. Does this graph tell you whether it's the school library or public library that the money is being raised for? _____

3. How many students want to have a car wash? _____

4. Which idea received the fewest votes? _____

5. Which fund-raiser do you think the students ended up doing?

   _____

Find a graph in a newspaper, magazine, or book and write a short paragraph that describes the graph's purpose.

WORDS WITH /ch/ AND /sh/

The /ch/ and /sh/ sound can be spelled in different ways, as in *lunch*, *dash*, *mention*, and *cello*. Use the clues to help you fill in the crossword puzzle. Each word has /ch/ or /sh/.

(crossword puzzle grid with decorative "ch" and "sh" lettering)

Across entries shown in grid:
- 2. _ _ _ n k
- 3. m (down clue marker)
- 4. c (down clue marker)
- 5. _ _ _ n g _
- 6. a d _ _ _ _ _
- 7. _ _ _ i c _ _
- 8. _ e l _ _
- 9. _ _ _ _ _

ACROSS

2. to grow smaller in size

3. to chew noisily

5. to make different

6. opposite of subtraction

7. decision

8. musical instrument related to the violin

9. plate

DOWN

1. facial feature below the mouth

3. to speak about

4. held tightly, like a fist

Write three words that start with /sh/ and three words that start with /ch/. Use each word in a funny sentence.

SPELLING PATTERNS

Write the word that fits each clue. All the words in each box will have some of the same letters—or the same spelling pattern.

Words with spelling pattern *-ime*

_____ It's worth ten cents.

_____ You measure it in seconds, minutes, and hours.

_____ It's a sour green fruit.

_____

Words with spelling pattern *-ank*

_____ a place to keep your pennies

_____ a joke played on someone

_____ made a very unpleasant odor

_____

Words with spelling pattern *-ide*

_____ to sit in a moving vehicle

_____ a woman who is newly married

_____ a feeling of self-respect

Think of four words that have the spelling pattern *-an*. Write a clue for each word and then give your puzzle to a classmate to solve.

BETWEEN THE LINES

Fill in the bubble next to the best answer. Then write the answer to the last question.

1. James prepared well for his first face-to-face meeting with the mayor because
   - (a) James wanted the mayor to like him.
   - (b) he wanted the mayor to take him seriously.
   - (c) his father would have been disappointed if he hadn't.

2. The town administrator said the place James had suggested for the new playground was too small. He probably
   - (a) expected James to stop and not continue his efforts.
   - (b) didn't want to listen to a kid.
   - (c) wanted to get back to his office.

3. Getting the story into the Miami newspaper helped James's cause because
   - (a) the mayor would not have helped him otherwise.
   - (b) James would have a good chance of writing for the paper.
   - (c) more people in the community learned about and supported his efforts.

4. James worked to get the mayor reelected because
   - (a) she listened to him and did what she could to help.
   - (b) his father was on the town council.
   - (c) he didn't like the other candidate.

5. What qualities does James have that make him a good leader?

   _____

   _____

   _____

Write a brief paragraph about what kind of job you think James Ale will have when he is older. Explain how you reached your conclusion.

INFORMATION: HERE, THERE, EVERYWHERE

Use one word from the word boxes to complete each sentence. You won't use all the words.

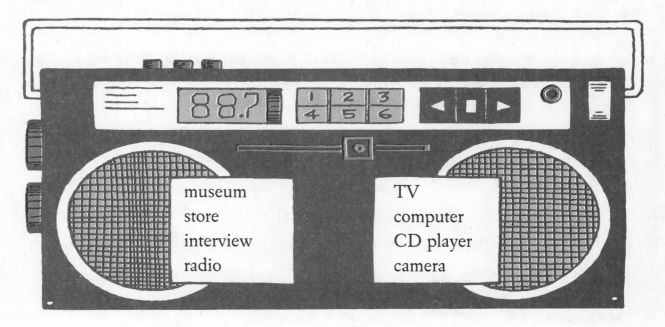

museum
store
interview
radio

TV
computer
CD player
camera

1. People driving in a car can get news on the _____.

2. One way to learn about how Native Americans lived long ago would be

   to watch a documentary on _____.

3. A _____ can record on-the-spot news, such as a fire in a building.

4. One of the best ways to learn about a person's job is to conduct an _____ with him or her.

5. A good way to become skillful at a new game, such as chess, is to practice it on a

   _____.

Suppose you wanted to tell someone about yourself and could not use print media. How might you present the information?

ANTONYMS

Read the following story. It doesn't make sense as it's written. Fix it by writing an antonym—or word with an opposite meaning—for each underlined word. The first one has been done for you.

> Clark got up (1) <u>late</u> in the morning and got dressed for school. Then he went (2) <u>upstairs</u> and ate some breakfast. When his stomach was (3) <u>empty</u>, he grabbed his books and closed the (4) <u>front</u> door. It was very (5) <u>hot</u> (6) <u>inside</u>. He decided he needed a (7) <u>light</u> coat. Clark rode his bicycle to school, because it was a (8) <u>slow</u> way to travel. Clark arrived (9) <u>after</u> 8:30, but the school doors were (10) <u>closed</u>. He said (11) <u>goodbye</u> to his teacher. Then he (12) <u>stood up</u> and waited for class to begin.

1. _____early_____   7. _____

2. _____   8. _____

3. _____   9. _____

4. _____   10. _____

5. _____   11. _____

6. _____   12. _____

EXTENSION Write a paragraph about your classroom. Use at least two pairs of antonyms.

DOING THE RIGHT THING

Fill in the bubble next to the best answer. Then explain why you chose that answer.

1. The theme of *Teammates* can be expressed in this way:
   - (a) Jackie Robinson was a great baseball player.
   - (b) It took courageous people to get others to accept African Americans into major league baseball.
   - (c) Crosley Field was a terrible place to play ball.

2. I chose this answer because _____

   _____

   _____

3. Another way to state the theme of *Teammates* is:
   - (a) Baseball is a great sport.
   - (b) Stand up for what you believe is right.
   - (c) The game must go on.

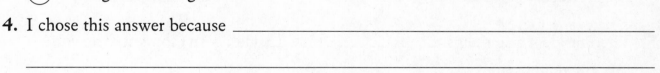

4. I chose this answer because _____

   _____

   _____

   _____

Think of a favorite book that you have read recently. In a few sentences, explain what you think the theme of the book is.

Name

TAKE ACTION

Choose the word from the box that best completes each sentence.

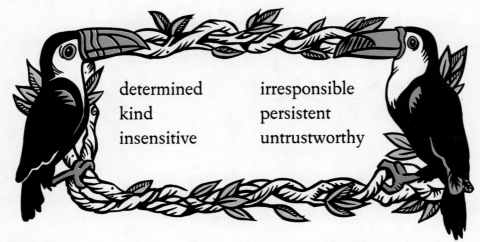

determined   irresponsible
kind   persistent
insensitive   untrustworthy

1. Omar Castillo is _____ to save the rainforest.

2. Don Miguel is a _____ man who cares about animals and the environment.

3. The governor seems to be _____ to the problem of the rainforest. He refuses to take Omar's fears seriously.

4. The President seems to be _____. He makes a promise he doesn't keep.

5. The President also seems _____. He doesn't think it is his job to save the rainforest.

6. Omar will continue to be _____ in his fight to save the rainforest.

THINK & WRITE

Think of a famous character from a book or movie. Make a list of adjectives that describe the character and see if your classmates can guess who it is.

WHAT'S YOUR ORDER?

**Number each sentence in the order the events occurred
in the story *Save My Rainforest*.**

_____ Omar realizes that the President is not to be believed.

_____ Omar has a birthday celebration.

_____ Omar and his father camp out in the *Zocalo*.

_____ Omar finds out about the earthquake in Mexico City.

_____ A restaurant owner turns Omar and his father away without giving them food.

_____ Omar's father gets blisters on his feet.

_____ Omar meets the governor.

_____ Omar and his father arrive at Tuxtla Gutiérrez.

_____ Omar sees the President.

_____ Omar and his father visit Don Miguel.

WHAT ARE THESE CHARACTERS LIKE?

Sometimes characters in a selection have strong emotions. As you read,
fill in the web to compare ways characters express their emotions.
Give specific examples.

CHARACTER: _____

_____

_____

_____

_____

_____

CHARACTER: _____

_____

_____

_____

_____

_____

EMOTIONS

CHARACTER: _____

_____

_____

_____

_____

_____

CHARACTER: _____

_____

_____

_____

_____

_____

CHARACTER CLUES

Fill in five clues about a character. Present them to the class one at a time. Speak slowly and clearly. How many clues does it take to guess the character?

Selection Title: _____

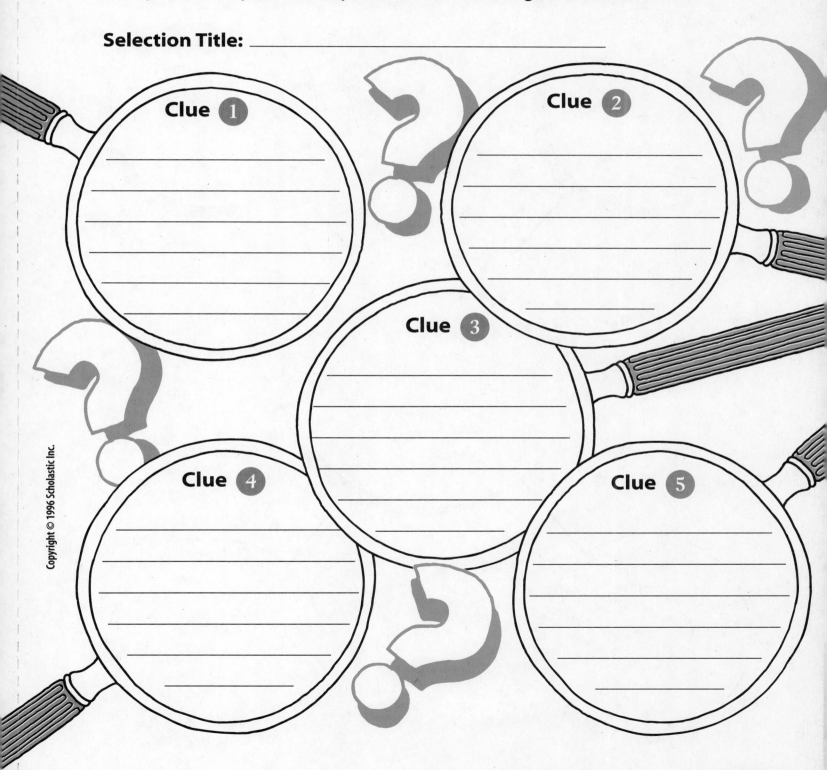

Clue ①

Clue ②

Clue ③

Clue ④

Clue ⑤

SEMANTIC MAP

Use the semantic map to brainstorm and record your ideas.

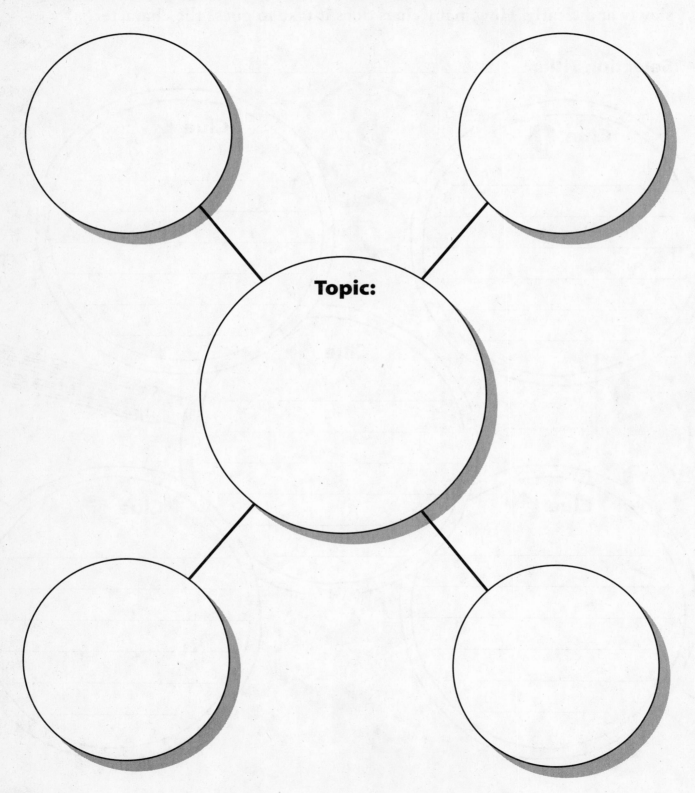

Topic: